YOUR TIME TO HEAL

Your Step-by-Step Guide from Grief to Healing

DORIS L. LANG

Copyright © 2007 by Doris L. Lang

Your Time To Heal
Your Step-by-Step Guide from Grief to Healing
by Doris L. Lang

Printed in the United States of America

ISBN 978-1-60266-789-1

All rights reserved solely by the author. The author guarantees all contents are original and do not infringe upon the legal rights of any other person or work. No part of this book may be reproduced in any form without the permission of the author. The views expressed in this book are not necessarily those of the publisher.

Unless otherwise indicated, Bible quotations are taken from the King James Version of the Bible. Copyright © 1988 by Thomas Nelson Publishers.

www.xulonpress.com

DEDICATION

I dedicate this book to my children
James Richard Deajon, Jr.
and
Candace Morgan Lang,
for your courage, your strength, and your love.

ACKNOWLEDGEMENTS

I am grateful for the support and advice of many friends and family members who made it possible for me to write this book. I would like to especially thank Percine Dorris, my dear friend since 1991; she opened her heart and home to me while I was writing this book. Her love, support and pearls of wisdom were invaluable to this project—I am so thankful for her generous spirit and the impact she has had upon my life.

I would like to thank and honor my friend and confidant for many years, Brenda Osborn, for being a friend who sticks closer than a brother. Her administrative expertise, loyalty, and commitment to the vision of this book were instrumental in seeing this project through to completion.

I want to thank my eighteen-year-old niece, Elaina Bell, who offered invaluable critiques for the book and, in doing so, discovered that she has a God-given gift as a copy editor.

A special thanks should go to all those who supported me and cheered me on during the writing of this book, including but not limited to Kenneth and Robbin Bell, Angie Cavese for helping with the final edit, Kay Coulter and Terri Walker for helping with editing and proofreading, Mary Allen and Rebecca La Chapelle for helping with some of the initial research for the book, and to my highly esteemed bosses, William S. Cabaniss, D.D.S. and Mark E. Falke, D.D.S., who allowed me the time off that I needed to write, and write, and write.

I would like to thank Eddie Smith, from the US Prayer Center, for his powerful seminar on writing a book and getting it published. His ministry provided a wealth of information about writing and publishing that came to me at just the right time.

And finally, to all of my family and friends who have not seen much of me while writing this book, thank you for being understanding and patient, and for genuinely believing the best in me.

Most of all, I would like to thank God for giving me the courage to write this book.

TABLE OF CONTENTS

FOREWORD xiii

LETTER TO READER xv

CHAPTER 1: THE MORNING OF 21

- The Day My Life Changed Forever

CHAPTER 2: QUESTIONING GOD 33

- Learn How to Seek God for Understanding about Your Loss
- Learn How to Maintain the Right Perspective about Suffering and Loss
- Learn How to Seek God for the Answers You Need
- Learn the Power of Acceptance

CHAPTER 3: PROCESSING GRIEF 57

- Learn What Grief Is All About, How to Process It, and What God Wants It to Produce in Your Life
- Learn How to Deal with Grief One Day at a Time
- Learn How Men Grieve Differently than Women
- Learn How to Help Friends and Families in Grief

CHAPTER 4: UNDERSTANDING GRIEF EMOTIONS 101

- Learn How to Identify and Resolve Painful Emotions Associated with Grief
- Learn How to Come to Terms with Issues from Your Past
- Learn How to Free Your Life from Negative Emotions
- Learn How to Overcome Fear

CHAPTER 5: HEALING DEEP WOUNDS 137

- Learn Why God Wants to Heal You from the Inside Out
- Learn Why Unresolved Hurts Can Keep You Stuck in Grief
- Learn What to Do to Free Yourself from Hurts of the Past

- Learn How Seeing Vision Can Help You Heal

CHAPTER 6: FORGIVING ALL.................................... 167

- Learn Why Forgiveness Is Your Master Key to Complete Healing and Freedom
- Learn What it Means to Forgive From the Heart
- Learn How to Free Your Life from Bitterness
- Learn Why Anger and Unforgiveness Can Keep You from Healing

CHAPTER 7: TRUSTING GOD...................................... 195

- Learn How to Maintain Your Faith after Loss
- Learn How Faith and Trust Can Unlock Doors to Your Future
- Learn How to Release Your Faith for a New Start in Life
- Learn How to Trust God in the Midst of Adversity

TRIBUTE: STEPHANIE'S STORY................................217
   APPENDIX: FATHER'S LOVE LETTER................ 227
   ADDENDUM I: POWER THOUGHTS 233
   ADDENDUM II: PRAYERS THAT HEAL A
      GRIEVING HEART 237
   SUGGESTED RESOURCES 247
   BIBLIOGRAPHY.. 251

FOREWORD

Life often brings with it unwanted hardships in many of the vital areas we pass through on our journey of growth. These areas include our social, economic, or personal interactions, and they can bear a full range of negative outcomes that are either undetectable to the individual, to ones that are so severe that the person involved is simply devastated.

I want you to know that hardships are no respecter of persons; to a child it can come from the loss of a loving pet; to a young person, the betrayal of a close friend or even personal injury; and to an adult a bad financial decision or the loss of a loved one from death or divorce. These are just a few examples, but the range of incidents that carry hardships into our lives is almost unlimited, and the degree of pain it carries is always very personal.

I recall the day when the news came that my grandfather had not returned home from a hunting trip and a mass of volunteers were out searching for him. I was only five years old at the time, and as an adult today, I can still remember vividly the series of events that unfolded. After two days of searching, my grandfather was found but he was barely alive with both knees broken from a hunting accident. He died en route to the hospital with my father accompanying him.

Although I was very young when the death of my grandfather occurred, I noticed the overwhelming pain that this unexpected loss caused my grandmother and all of his twelve children. On reading the manuscript for this book, I wished that it were available for my relatives at that time long ago when they experienced the loss of someone so dear to them.

Doris Lang writes on the subject of dealing with grief generated from hardships and loss with extraordinary maturity based on personal experience. Many deny or ignore the possibility of full recovery from devastating loss, but in this book you will be taken on a step-by-step journey to recovery.

This book is a presentation of how God will help you overcome your grief. It is carefully thought through, extremely practical, and compellingly readable. I recommend you use this book as a tool to victory for yourself or anyone you know that is stuck in grief from a difficult and painful loss.

Kenneth L. Bell
Businessman/Entrepreneur/IBM
Austin, TX

LETTER TO READER

I applaud you if you have picked up this book to read about a subject that is universal, yet a subject that many people avoid as much as possible. Experiencing any type of loss can be very painful and extremely personal. No one is ever prepared for the intense despair and hopelessness that loss brings, the painful process of grieving that follows, or the long, rocky road back to reality.

During the first few months after the loss of my daughter, I received beautiful cards and gifts from friends and relatives sending their love and condolences. Some of what I received were books written specifically about loss and grief. At first I was hesitant to read about a subject that had been forced into my life, but eventually I did begin reading, hoping to find something that would help me to get through the grieving process.

What I found were literally volumes of written material on the subject of grief. The only problem is that you read about grief with your head, but grief is in your heart and only

God can heal a broken heart. On the other hand, some of what I read was very beneficial and really helped to comfort me. Most grievers would agree that the process of grieving itself is very unique for each individual.

However, there is yet another aspect of grief that is applicable to everyone. No matter how unique your situation may be, or how much you try to expedite your own recovery through education, you must still go through the process of grieving. Because we all handle grief very differently, it is possible to get trapped in the grief process without realizing what has happened.

One thing for sure—there is no microwave approach to the process. To my knowledge, no shortcuts exist. The only way through it is to just go through it. My prayer is that the information in this book will help you safely navigate your way through the healing process and beyond.

For a long time, I questioned whether I would ever get out from under the heavy weight of grief, but the good news is that you can and you will! I am living proof that you can overcome. Yes, you can survive the traumatic loss of a loved one, or any traumatic loss, and continue to live a purposeful and peaceful life.

This book is about overcoming grief; it's about thinking right; it's about understanding the process; it's about healing; it's about honesty; it's about forgiveness; and it's about starting over again. If you are hurting and searching for something to help you heal from grief, this book was written as a tool to help you overcome. It will help you come to terms with, put closure on, accept, process, and resolve the hurt and pain that is in your life because of a tragic loss.

Every chapter in this grief guidebook is a necessary step I had to take or a mental crossing I had to make on the road to full recovery. The life principles that I have learned through my walk with God are those that I share with you in this book. I sincerely hope that these proven principles, combined with my insights on life-lessons learned, would speak louder to you than the pain you may be going through even now.

Each chapter focuses on the toughest areas of challenge you may encounter, and presents solutions and suggestions to help you overcome each and every one of them. Consider each chapter's wisdom in the light of where you are in the process of grieving, and then carefully apply a nugget of truth to your situation. As you do, please allow God to make it personal to you as He pours healing and wholeness into your heart.

I pray that your loss (of whatever magnitude you have experienced) will not destroy you but will ultimately bring you to a life of greater freedom, times of refreshing, and rebirthing of your deepest desires and dreams because this is *your time to heal*!

I begin with the day my life changed forever . . .

Doris L. Lang

> **To every thing there is a season, and a time to every purpose under the heaven.**
>
> **Ecclesiastes 3:1**

Chapter One

THE MORNING OF

The Day My Life Changed Forever

I walked by my daughter's bedroom and although I was not fully awake, I noticed that she was still asleep. Her mouth was slightly open, as mine often is when I am in a deep sleep or when I am sleeping on my back.

Stephanie was sleeping on her back, her right arm was leaning over the right side of the bed, and she was holding a glass of water in her right hand. Her left arm was spread open across the other side of the bed and she was holding her Bible in her left hand. It appeared that she had been reading late and fell asleep.

As I walked by, I thought to myself: *that is a strange position to fall asleep in—she must have been exhausted last night*. I knew she had been really tired and not feeling well since our recent trip to Europe, and that she had been up late the night before grading papers. I remember her telling me earlier in the day, "Mom, I'm going to stay in today because I really need to get caught up with all this paperwork from school."

Somehow I could not get out of my mind the way she was lying in her bed. By the time I reached the bathroom, it dawned on me that something was wrong—terribly wrong.

Within seconds I instinctively knew what it was—Stephanie was dead!

It was on that bright and sunny day around 7:00 a.m., on Sunday, March 26, 2000, that my life changed forever. I had fallen asleep on the living room couch the night before, something I did quite often. It was the start of our typical Sunday morning ritual: get ready for church, go to church, go home afterwards for lunch or eat out, then hopefully home again for a short nap, and back to church around 6:30 p.m. for the evening service.

But my daughter was dead!

Another part of me thought, *she can't be; she just can't be!* There was no time to process all of the thoughts rushing through my mind, I had to hurry into her bedroom and face my worst fears. From that point on, everything is a blur. Rushing into her room, I called out to her very firmly, "Stephanie, wake up! It's time to go to church!"

I noticed again the Bible in one hand, the glass of water in the other. My mind was racing—seeing her that way. What my mind had realized almost immediately, my heart totally rejected.

I took the glass of water out of her hand and sat it down on the nearby dresser. When I touched her, she felt cold and a little stiff, but I continued to pull her upper body toward me, and her head close to my chest, my voice trembling with fear, "Stephanie, wake up!" I called out to her again, even more desperately, "Stephanie! Stephanie! Stephanie! Wake Up! Wake Up!"

She did not respond.

Then I lowered her head back onto her pillow and ran as fast as I could to the kitchen for orange juice. It was what I gave her whenever she started to become sick. For a diabetic, sugar activates their insulin, which in turn determines their energy level. She had been at the point of unconsciousness many times before, and during those close calls, orange juice had always been beneficial. I was sure that orange juice in her system would work again. This time should be no different.

I ran back to her bedroom and called out, almost pleading with her, "Drink the orange juice, Stephanie, please drink the orange juice!" Since she still did not respond, I decided to force some orange juice into her mouth, and then I closed her lips together, so that perhaps the orange juice would go down her throat.

But the orange juice would not go down—instead it ran down her chin, her neck, and onto the pillowcase. I felt stupid and helpless and finally gave up on the orange juice. Total reality had not set in that she was dead. All I knew was that I had to keep trying to revive her. I could not give up!

Next, I ran frantically to her bathroom looking for medicine, her insulin, anything I could find to revive her, all the while knowing that every second was critical. I ran back to the living room, picked up the phone, and called for emergency help.

After I called 9-1-1, I then called my friend and coworker, James, and I called my pastors.

I told them that something was wrong with Stephanie and she was not responding. I asked them to come as quickly as they could and to please pray. There were others to call but there was no time.

I was almost out of breath, not just from running back and forth, but mainly from the sheer madness of it all.

No one that I had phoned, including the paramedics, had arrived yet; and time was running out. I called James a second time and said, "Come *now* James, I need you *now*!" That is when he informed me that he was on his way and would be there within minutes.

But I was still alone and I could not wait any longer—I had to do something. My last desperate attempt to revive Stephanie was to raise her from the dead. Surely, God would do a miracle for me! I laid my hands on her body and prayed, "In the name of Jesus, I command you, Stephanie, to come back into your body. Spirit of death, get off of my daughter in

Jesus' name." I waited, but nothing happened. Then I prayed again, this time even louder.

As I prayed, I remember feeling stupid, almost as if I had prayed the wrong prayer. I thought of all the times in the past that I had prayed for others, yet on that day, I had no faith to pray. Not only that, but I could not sense the presence of God—it was as if all of Heaven went with Stephanie, and I had been left in the dark.

About that time I heard a knock on the front door. I ran as fast as I could and opened the door—it was James! I was so glad to see him. I considered him to be a great man of faith, and I knew that together we would pray for Stephanie, and she would be healed. He followed me toward Stephanie's bedroom while I frantically filled him in on all the details of what happened.

When we got to her bedroom door, he said, "Just give me a minute." He went in alone.

I trusted James without reservation—he was over hospital visitation at our church. When he prayed for the sick, he had the gift of faith to see them healed. God had done miracles for others through his prayers. Many years before, his own wife had come out of an eight-day coma after James had prayed for her. Even the doctors agreed that her healing was nothing short of a miracle.

I had not cried yet, but as I waited in the hallway for James to come out of her room, tears began to fall. I began crying, but a part of me was afraid to really let go and cry the amount of tears I wanted to cry. I wanted to scream. I wanted to scream and never stop screaming, but in reality, there was no life in me to cry or to scream—something inside me died that day.

Then I heard James say as he came out into the hallway, "There's nothing we can do—she's dead." I responded immediately, almost in a rebuke, "No, she's not dead—we have to pray for her, James—we can't give up!"

I was still crying as he grabbed my arms, shook me forcefully as if to shake me back into reality, and then said very firmly, "Doris, she's dead! There is nothing else we can do!"

In almost the same breath, he hugged me, now crying himself. Then he said tenderly, "When I was in the room praying for her, I sensed the Lord saying, 'It's okay. She's with me now.'"

James continued to try and reason with me, "Doris, she's in Heaven. She's with Jesus. She died with the peace of God on her face—there was no apparent struggle. She saw the glory of God and stepped into eternity."

That was not what I wanted to hear! I wanted him to come out of Stephanie's bedroom with her by his side, both of them leaping and jumping and praising God. I wanted to hear him say that God had healed her completely—that God had breathed the breath of life back into her lungs. I wanted to be able to say, "Devil, you took your best shot, but your best shot was not good enough!"

I wanted to hold my daughter in my arms, hug her tight, kiss her cheeks, and tell her how much I loved her. I wanted to tell her how brave she had been throughout her entire life. I wanted to tell her how proud I was of her and how everything was going to be alright.

James began to minister to me about Heaven, but at that time I could not receive what he was saying. He tried his best to console me that day. I was listening and agreeing, but even though I knew that what he was saying was true, it did not make any difference to me, because Stephanie was gone—my daughter was dead!

As a minister, I had given these same words of encouragement to others who had lost loved ones, but for me, words alone would not suffice for the tragedy that had just occurred. The more James talked, almost pleading with me, the more difficult it became to look into his eyes. I could only look away and cry. I thought of how senseless it was for her to die this way.

Stephanie had big dreams for her life. She wanted to marry and have children one day. She also wanted to do great things for God. All of her hopes and dreams had been destroyed! The finality of what had happened was just too much to deal with—I felt frozen and dead on the inside—there where no emotions to feel or tears to cry.

All I could think of was about all those years in ministry, all those years of learning the Word of God, all the years of serving God, all the years of believing for Stephanie's healing, and now—just like that—she was dead. I did not see it coming; I was blindsided. It felt as if time had stopped.

When the paramedics arrived, I was not allowed to go into Stephanie's room while they examined her and assessed the situation for any foul play.

Then, from down the hallway, I heard them say, "DOA." I repeated it almost in a whisper to myself, "Dead on arrival." It was true—she was dead. I had to accept it. I had to face it. All my hopes for a miracle had been totally crushed.

Once foul play had been ruled out, the paramedics called the coroner's office to pick up Stephanie's body and pronounce her legally dead. My heart sank! With every pronouncement, it felt like huge daggers shooting through my heart, as I spiraled deeper and deeper into an invisible black hole of nothingness and numbness.

As news of Stephanie's death spread, friends and relatives started gathering at our home. My pastors arrived. They hugged me and searched for the right words to say. But what could anyone say? Words seemed useless that day.

Once all the official paperwork was completed, my pastors followed me into Stephanie's room so I could see her once more and say my final good-bye. But I could not say good-bye because the real Stephanie was not there anymore—and because I just could not say the words.

I was not ready to say good-bye!

Men from the coroner's office took Stephanie's body from our home, tightly zipped and tucked away in a black vinyl bag. I looked on in horror, disbelief, and shock as they wheeled her body away, and as my heart was ripping apart.

While they were removing her body, my friends huddled close around me like a protective shield, perhaps thinking I would really lose it now. But I didn't—I couldn't—there was nothing there. All I felt was deep sadness and emptiness. *Oh God, if I could just reverse the clock, maybe I could have helped Stephanie in her struggle that night and she would still be alive today.*

But that is now in the past, and nothing can change what happened that Sunday morning. On a clear, sunny day around 10:00 a.m., my twenty-five-year-old daughter, Stephanie Renee Deajon, was pronounced dead in our home. She had gone into a diabetic coma in the middle of the night, and died around 3:00 a.m. on the morning of March 26, 2000.

That was the day my life changed forever.

But I would not have you to be ignorant, brethren, concerning them which are asleep, that ye sorrow not, even as others which have no hope. For if we believe that Jesus died and rose again, even so them also which sleep in Jesus will God bring with him. For this we say unto you by the word of the Lord, that we which are alive and remain unto the coming of the Lord shall not prevent them which are asleep. For the Lord himself shall descend from heaven with a shout, with the voice of the archangel, and with the trump of God: and the dead in Christ shall rise first: Then we which are alive and remain shall be caught up together with them in the clouds, to meet the Lord in the air: and so shall we ever be with the Lord. Wherefore comfort one another with these words.

1 Thessalonians 4:13-18

JOURNAL NOTES

Chapter Two

QUESTIONING GOD

The secret things belong unto the LORD our God: but those things which are revealed belong unto us and to our children forever, that we may do all the words of this law. Deuteronomy 29:29

WHY LORD WHY?

As easy as it would have been to fall apart, I had to be strong. There were funeral arrangements to be made, and many other decisions to contemplate before facing family and friends at my daughter's memorial service. What did God want to say to all of us about Stephanie's death? As her mother, what should I say?

As I was preparing my speech for her home-going service, I prayed about the specifics of what the Lord would have me to share. Speaking at her funeral would be difficult, but I wanted to say something worthwhile that would honor her memory. My message to all who knew and loved Stephanie needed to be encouraging and uplifting, and spoken in faith, opposed to a message spoken strictly from my emotions.

The first impression I received from the Lord had to do with the question of *why*. This is probably the most commonly asked question when someone dies, or when any type of catastrophic event has occurred in someone's life. But the real question to ask is not *why,* but *what*. Instead of asking why Stephanie died, those of us who were left behind should ask ourselves, "What are we going to do with our lives?" Would we choose to give up? Would we become bitter or lose faith in God?

My daughter's death was now part of my past, but I had to choose what my future would be like now that she was gone. The days ahead should not be spent on questions that had no answers, but instead, it should be spent on deciding what I would do with my time left here on earth. Stephanie had lived out her number of days; she had loved God and lived an honorable life.

The question to ask was how would those of us who were left behind live out the rest of our days? Would we continue to fulfill the assignment and call of God upon our lives? Would we continue to serve God?

The other word the Lord gave me to share was about not quitting. I could not give up on life, because it would not bring honor to Stephanie's memory or to the Kingdom of God. Stephanie would not have wanted her death to destroy my faith and future, nor the faith and future of anyone else. She would want us to continue on with our lives and to do great things for God—which was always the desire of her heart.

I also shared from John 12:24, where Jesus said, "Verily, verily, I say unto you, Except a corn of wheat fall into the ground and die, it abideth alone: but if it die, it bringeth forth much fruit." The Lord prompted me to claim this scripture by faith and believe that Stephanie's life was like that grain of wheat in the Book of John that, once sown into spiritual soil, would eventually produce a rich harvest.

She was not to be considered another statistic, nor would she be considered a casualty of war. Her life had purpose, meaning, and impact, even after death.

By faith, I could choose to believe that her life had been sown like a seed, or I could resign myself to the fact that her death was just unfortunate and tragic. Stephanie had impacted many lives during her brief twenty-five years. I decided to exercise my faith in God to see the far-reaching results that her life would have as time went on.

The words I spoke at Stephanie's funeral became a pointer that I kept before me. When the shock of her death wore off and I began experiencing the full force of grief, I continued to recall these words year after year, using them as an inspiration to propel me onward.

Any type of devastating loss opens a Pandora's Box of questions, some of which may go a lifetime without being answered. As time progresses and questions still remain unanswered, many people simply give up. They become hopeless, negative, angry, or backslidden because they feel that life has dealt them a bad hand.

They never grow beyond the pain of their loss, and in many instances, never reach their full potential in life. Sometimes they are never willing to trust God again, which only compounds the tragedy of their initial loss.

It is not wrong to question God. He wants you to take your most distressing questions to Him. However, I have found that if you ask God to answer your questions, you must be prepared to receive the answer(s) that He gives you.

One plaguing question that I had was *how could Stephanie have died from diabetes? Most people live very long and productive lives with this disease.* There had to be a better explanation for her death than succumbing to a disease that can be easily managed with diet, exercise, and insulin.

I could not dismiss the nagging thought that her death may have been caused by something other than a diabetic coma. Even though I questioned the legitimacy of how she died, I knew that diabetes was a life-threatening disease with the potential to kill.

There was no reason to feel that something mysterious had happened—the autopsy revealed that a diabetic coma was the cause of death.

Once the autopsy report came back, I was able to lay aside my uncertainties about how she died, realizing that the doubts

I had in my mind about her death were normal questions that any grieving parent would have had in the same situation.

THE SECRET THING

As I was crying out to God, He began to speak to my heart about Stephanie's death and I heard on the inside, "The secret things belong to the Lord." The Lord helped me to understand that some situations we experience, including the losses we face in life, will never be fully understood on this side of eternity. God will not reveal them to you because they do not belong to you. They belong to God. Your Heavenly Father reserves the right to decide what He will or will not reveal to man. I began to think about the meaning of Deuteronomy 29:29 in natural terms. Just as a wise parent may withhold particular information from a child in that child's best interest, God does the same with His children.

Parents withhold information from their children for various reasons. Perhaps the child is not mature enough to handle a certain subject matter. There are some things that young children do not need to know, simply because they are adult matters. In the same way, there are some things that man does not need to know, simply because they are God matters. God knows what is best for His children and He always has your best interest at heart. He holds the key to everything and He alone knows the future. As a Christian, it is important that you trust Him implicitly with every perplexing question you have, and every difficult experience you face in life.

Even Jesus did not directly answer all of the disciples' questions as they desired them to be answered. When they asked the resurrected Christ when the Kingdom would be restored to Israel, His answer probably surprised them. In Acts 1:7, Jesus answered, "It is not for you to know the times or the seasons, which the Father hath put in his own power."

What Jesus was saying is that only God knows the times when the kingdom will be restored to Israel. It is not for man to know. The disciples did not continue to question Him or become offended because He did not give them the answer that they wanted to hear. They accepted the answer given to them, trusting His wisdom even though they may not have understood why.

What the disciples were certain of, however, was that Jesus would not lie to them.

Proverbs 3:5-6,8 says to, "Trust in the LORD with all thine heart; and lean not unto thine own understanding. In all thy ways acknowledge him, and he shall direct thy paths. It shall be health to thy navel and marrow to thy bones." This verse instructs you to acknowledge God, and in doing so, He promises to direct your life in a healthy way. What does it mean in practical terms to acknowledge Him?

- Acknowledging Him means that, although you do not have all the answers, you are willing to trust and seek the One who does.
- Acknowledging Him means you understand that your Heavenly Father knows best, and you are willing to continually yield to Him in what is best for your life.
- Acknowledging Him means you trust the path that God has set for you, even though you may not see the full picture of what lies ahead in your future.
- Acknowledging Him means that you are willing to release control of your life to a sovereign God.
- Acknowledging Him means that you are willing to submit to God without hesitation, because you know that no matter what happens, everything will eventually "…work together for good to them that love God, to them who are the called according to his purpose." (Romans 8:28)

When you arrive at this place in your heart, you will stop tormenting yourself with unanswered questions. You will also be able to enter God's rest, which is only achieved by having faith in Him. Hebrews 4:9-10 confirms that, "There remaineth therefore a rest to the people of God. For he that is entered into his rest, he also hath ceased from his own works, as God did from his."

When you are at rest, you can better receive and accept the answers that God does give you. The Holy Spirit will give you an inner peace that will help you embrace from God what you need to know, when you need to know it. When this happens, you stop struggling with issues that have no immediate answers. More importantly, you stop striving and stressing out over things in your life that cannot be changed, or things about which an answer cannot be given.

ENTERING INTO GOD'S PRESENCE

One of the best solutions for anxiety and stress is to enter into the Lord's presence with no agenda except to be with your Creator, the One who loves you with an everlasting love. When you are in God's presence, it becomes so easy to forget about the pressing matters of life. It is only in His presence that you can reach a place of contentment and peace, where having all the answers about your loss is no longer an issue. Once you are in His presence, your mind will no longer be plagued by those unanswered questions.

No outside force, including Satan himself, can follow you into the presence of God. When your spirit becomes joined with God, all other distractions fade away. Questions that gnaw at us for answers (when outside of the presence of God) originate from our souls. Your soul is very demanding, but it must be continually brought under subjection to your spirit in order for peace to rule and reign in your heart and mind.

HE IS SOVEREIGN

The key to victory in this area is to acknowledge that God is sovereign. The Lord should have the final say in your life if you are surrendered to His Lordship. One of the most important times to acknowledge His sovereignty is when you feel that what happened to you or to your deceased loved one was not right, not fair, or that it was unjust.

This dilemma in questioning God reminds me of Job's struggle in the Bible. Job had suffered the loss of his children, his finances, and was battling a terrible skin disease when the issue of trusting God became paramount. Job finally reached a point in all of his questioning, murmuring, and suffering where he realized that it was the issue of God's sovereignty that he needed to resolve in his heart, not the question of why he was suffering.

Job knew that God alone reserved the supreme right to order the universe, and in particular, Job's life. Once he was able to fully accept his situation, he knew that he needed to repent for questioning God. Unlike his friends, Job did not assume that God had to come down to his level, answer all of his questions, and respond to all of his fears. (See Job 42:1-7.)

Questioning God can be a sign of doubt and unbelief, and can indicate a person's lack of trust in God the Father. Job knew in his heart that he had misjudged God's faithfulness to him, and in doing so, had not shown absolute trust in the God he loved. Questioning God is a natural response at first, but at some point, the questions have to be laid at His feet and you must wait on God to reveal what He chooses to reveal. This is one way you enter into His rest.

The Lord knows the heart of man, and He knew Job was truly sorry for his fearful response. Unfortunately, Job's three comfortless friends never saw the need to repent, even though they were also guilty of the same. In the Old Testament, God addressed the prophet Jeremiah and said,

> Therefore thus says the Lord [to Jeremiah]: If you return [and give up this mistaken tone of distrust and despair], then I will give you again a settled place of quiet and safety, and you will be My minister; and if you separate the precious from the vile [cleansing your own heart from unworthy and unwarranted suspicions concerning God's faithfulness], you shall be My mouthpiece. Jeremiah 15:19 (AMP)

If you give up your need to question things, the Lord promises to bring you to a place of peace and safety. What you need more than an answer is to be comforted by the God of all comforts. God cannot do what He wants in your life if you are unwilling to trust Him when tragedy and disaster strikes. My experience has taught me that God is not the author of the bad things that may happen in a person's life. However, God will take the opportunity to stretch your faith and trust in Him in the midst of sickness, trials, and tribulations.

Job's friends were full of doubt and unbelief about God, and they had many suspicions about possible sin in Job's life. His friends had the wrong view about Job's suffering, but they were no different than many Christians are today. Most Christians believe that when something tragic happens in a person's life, that person must have committed a sin; and therefore, God is judging that individual. Neither of these assumptions, however, was the case with Job. His friends completely misjudged both God and Job.

They were unable to spiritually discern what was taking place in Job's life. They did not understand how God was working behind the scenes in Job's life. Eventually, the Lord confronted Job's friend Eliphaz by saying, " . . . for ye have not spoken of me the thing that is right, as my servant Job hath." (Job 42:7)

However, Job concluded that God was in control—that God was sovereign. Job came to realize that God knew what He was doing and did not need to explain Himself to Job. Therefore, Job proved his trust in God by accepting what he did not understand. Job put his trust in God's faithfulness and trustworthiness instead of his circumstances. This was his place of victory and breakthrough in coming to terms with his sickness and loss. For Job, the new revelation released the grace, strength and healing power of God in his situation.

Even though his friends had missed it, Job had not. When Job made the decision to trust God despite what he was going through and the pain he was suffering, he was healed instantly. When you reach a place where you can accept your loss without reservations, and at the same time, you can accept the unwelcome changes that came into your life because of your loss, then healing and restoration will break forth for you. True acceptance of your circumstances produces strength and peace and will always lead to some type of significant breakthrough in your life.

Another aspect to consider when you have questions about a suffered loss is that our earthly perspective is limited. I Corinthians 13:12 states, ". . . for now we see through a glass darkly; but then face to face: now I know in part; but then shall I know even as also I am known."

This scripture implies that you will never have perfect comprehension and understanding of everything in this earthly life. Not until you see Jesus face to face will you know all things, for then you will be like Him.

When you become like Him, you will be known and will see all things as they really are. You can be at peace with this reality if you choose to let God have control of your life, and if you place your faith in His Word, for only His Words produce true life and peace (John 6:63).

OVERANALYZING YOUR LOSS

Overanalyzing can lead to what is sometimes known as analysis paralysis, causing you to stay stuck in grief or bound to issues from your past. This state of mind occurs when the over-analysis of your circumstances becomes counterproductive to your healing. Obviously, there are some details about your loss that you seek answers to, but when you become consumed, obsessed, or driven in this area, it is very difficult to move forward in the grieving process.

For instance, in the case of my daughter's death, although the autopsy report documented that Stephanie passed away after slipping into a diabetic coma, it was unacceptable to me. I needed something more tangible and concrete, something that would better justify her death.

The fact is, that nothing anyone could say, or do, or discover would ever be able to justify Stephanie's death. The issue was not about having all of the answers. My problem was in not being able to accept the reality of her death.

This unending quest of asking questions that had no immediate answers became a useless exercise that actually slowed down my recovery. It was not until I was able to accept my loss with total abandonment that I began to heal.

ABANDONMENT

Being able to abandon yourself to God by completely accepting the reality of your loss is extremely significant to your healing. According to Madame Guyon in her classic book, *Experiencing the Depths of Jesus Christ,*

> Abandonment is practiced by continually losing your own will in the will of God. It is forgetting your past; it is leaving your future in His hands; it is devoting the present fully and completely to your Lord. Abandonment is being satisfied with the present moment, no matter what the moment contains. You are satisfied because you know that whatever that moment has, it contains—in that instant—God's eternal plan for you.[1]

ACCEPTANCE

When you lose your will into the will of the Father, you accept everything that comes into your life—whether good or bad—whether you understand it or not—knowing that it has been filtered by your Heavenly Father with you, His child, in mind. He has a provision for you. He has a plan for your life. He has a pathway out of your deepest darkness.

With these truths in mind, allow the Holy Spirit to bring you to a place where abandonment to God and contentment with your circumstances becomes your new reality.

The plain truth is that what happened *happened.* It cannot be undone. It cannot be changed. It cannot be reversed. Accepting what you cannot change is imperative to your healing, or your grief journey will never end. The

Serenity Prayer sums it up quite well. Ask God to grant you the serenity to accept the things you cannot change; courage to change the things you can; and the wisdom to know the difference.[2]

STOP QUESTIONING, START BELIEVING

Like anyone else who has experienced a tragic loss, I assumed that if I could get all of my questions answered to my liking, it would at some point enable me to accept the loss of my daughter. But I was simply trapped in a vicious cycle—one question leading to another question, leading to another question—the list of questions never ended!

In spite of this merry-go-round of questions, I was determined that the loss of my daughter would not prevent me from fulfilling the Lord's purpose for my life. Therefore, I pressed through all the confusion I experienced over her death with sheer determination and willpower.

Having the right perspective became very important to my recovery from grief. My decision to look at what had happened in a different light helped me to embrace the process of grief, make the necessary changes and adjustments along the way, and continue to believe God for His best in my life. I decided that going on with God would be my way of honoring my daughter's memory.

Instead of focusing on the past, I began seeking God in order to discover what new things He wanted to do in my life. I knew that my healing would only come as I moved forward and as I refused to look back. In Jeremiah 29:11 (NIV), the Lord said, "For I know the plans I have for you,' declares the LORD, 'plans to prosper you and not to harm you, plans to give you hope and a future." God wants to heal the pain in your life and He wants to give you a new start—a fresh new customized beginning—to turn a new page and chapter in your life. But you must want this new life in order to receive it from God.

You must trust that your future will brighten again. Proverbs 4:18 states that, " . . . the path of the righteous shines brighter and brighter like the noonday sun."

FOCUS ON THE KNOWN

Focusing on the known instead of the unknown would become my pathway to healing. Many of my questions did get answered over time. What I do know about Stephanie's death, based on the Word of God, and what the Holy Spirit revealed to me, began with a settled knowledge in my heart that Stephanie was in Heaven.

I tend to agree with my friend Percine who had this to say about Heaven, "When you are dealing specifically with the death of a loved one where you do not know for sure that they are in Heaven, I believe this is one of those areas that is best left in the Lord's hands. In this life, you will not always have a suitable answer for every crisis you face. What God desires is a heart attitude that trusts in Him wholeheartedly. He desires that you do not lean to or trust your own understanding on the matter. God's ways are not our ways and His thoughts are not our thoughts. The answers to many of your questions should be left to His discretion."

The Bible is very clear about what happens to a believer after physical death occurs. Jesus said,

> Let not your heart be troubled: ye believe in God, believe also in me. In my Father's house are many mansions: if it were not so, I would have told you. I go to prepare a place for you. And if I go and prepare a place for you, I will come again, and receive you unto myself; that where I am, there ye may be also. (John 14:1-3)

Now that you know what your future in Christ holds, refuse to allow tragedy of any kind to ever bring you to a point of hopelessness, because Christ in you is that expectant hope of glory. (Colossians 1:27) When Christ lives in your heart, there is a river of hope that abides within you at all times.

This river of hope never stagnates and it never runs dry. Because of your loss, you may feel dry and empty on the inside, but that river can be released over and over again as you focus your heart toward God with expressions of love and trust in Him and His goodness.

In my worst period of grieving, I never quit (even though I sometimes wanted to) because that blessed, tangible, living hope inside of me refused to give up!

Jesus said in John 7:37-38, " . . . If any man thirst, let him come unto me, and drink. He that believeth on me, as the scripture hath said, out of his belly shall flow rivers of living water."

DEATH IS NOT THE END

Sometimes people fear what they do not understand. Consequently, many people fear death. However, there should be no fear in dying for those who are in Christ Jesus because death is not the end. Jesus said in John 11:25-26, "...I am the resurrection, and the life: he that believeth in me, though he were dead, yet shall he live: And whosoever liveth and believeth in me shall never die." If a person believes in Christ, when he dies his spirit will go to be with Jesus. Even though your physical body will cease to function when you die, your spirit man continues to live forever. For the believer, death is not the end but the beginning of eternal life in Christ.

If you have accepted Jesus Christ as your Lord and Savior, there is an exchange that takes place when you die. I think of it this way: at the instant of your last breath here on earth, you leave your earthly residence for your new residence in Heaven. You inhale on earth and exhale in Heaven, all in the same breath. The Apostle Paul said in 2 Corinthians 5:8, "We are confident, I say, and willing rather to be absent from the body, and to be present with the Lord."

The very instant a Christian dies, he or she is ushered into the presence of God. You go from earth to Heaven, with no stops in between. Therefore, death is not a demotion, but a promotion. That is why the Apostle Paul said, "For to me, to live is Christ, and to die is gain." (Philippians 1:21)

Knowing that death is not the end should keep a believer from being consumed with grief or from wanting to end his or her own life when a loved one dies. No mater what the manner of death was, your pain and grief should not destroy you but rather propel you forward and move you closer to God. The Lord will customize a new life for you. Do not give up because one day you will laugh and smile again!

SUMMING IT UP

As you are recovering from grief, whatever the Lord reveals to you concerning the death of your loved one, and in whatever way He chooses to reveal it, hold on to His words as very dear and precious. Write them in a journal or a book of remembrance. You can refer to them later as encouragement to yourself, or God may use what He has shown you to later comfort and help someone else who may be struggling to find answers about a loss.

My life is a prime example of someone who, through the grace of God, found strength to go on in spite of how deeply I was hurting and longing to see my daughter. Whether your loss is from the death of a loved one, or you have suffered some other devastating loss, you can go on in spite of how many questions have not been answered, or may never get answered on this side of eternity.

My final advice in seeking God for answers is this: Ask your questions, find out what you can, allow the Lord to reveal what He wants in His way and in His timing. Look to the Holy Scriptures for truth and comfort; let others love you and help you; but in the end, know that your lost loved ones in the Lord are with HIM—and they are in your future.

And what you do not know, release it to God, knowing that He does know and that is good enough for you.

No matter what type of loss you have endured, remember God's promises to you, for they are all yes and amen (I Corinthians 1:20).

As you progress through grief, you will begin to heal, you will have more clarity, and closure will come. As I close out this chapter, let me pray for you. *Lord, I pray that the person reading this chapter is able to completely lay aside every agonizing question in their heart. I pray that their grief will not consume them or make them wish that they were dead. I pray they will instead lean upon You for comfort, for love, and for peace of mind. Holy Spirit, comfort them in a way that they will know beyond a shadow of a doubt that they have been touched by God, in Jesus' name. Amen.*

Behold, I show you a mystery; We shall not all sleep, but we shall all be changed, in a moment, in the twinkling of an eye, at the last trump: for the trumpet shall sound, and the dead shall be raised incorruptible, and we shall be changed. For this corruptible must put on incorruption, and this mortal must put on immortality. So when this corruptible shall have put on incorruption, and this mortal shall have put on immortality, then shall be brought to pass the saying that is written, 'Death is swallowed up in victory. O death, where is thy sting? O grave, where is thy victory? I Corinthians 15:51-55

QUESTIONING GOD PRAYER

Dear Heavenly Father,

You said in Your Word to ask, seek, and knock. I ask You today to give me understanding about what happened. Help me to see what happened through Your eyes of love and not through the pain and heartache that I am feeling.

You said in Your Word that I could have the knowledge of your will with all spiritual wisdom and understanding. Lord, I ask for wisdom today, in everything that I do and say. I confess that Your Word is a lamp unto my feet and a light unto my path.

Lord, give me peace in my heart. I do acknowledge that You are Sovereign. Help me to accept my loss. Help me to trust and accept the things that I do not understand.

Open my eyes to see what You see, to hear what You hear, to say what You say, and to think Your thoughts.

Fill me with Your Holy Spirit today. I receive Your grace, Your understanding, Your peace, Your love, and Your strength, in Jesus' name. Amen.

JOURNAL NOTES

Chapter Three

PROCESSING GRIEF

Then Job replied: If only my anguish could be weighed and all my misery be placed on the scales. It would surely outweigh the sand of the seas—no wonder my words have been impetuous. Job 6:1-3 (NIV)

LOSING A SON

No matter how many questions you are left with about your loss, you must face the pain of grief like the mother in this next story. With great courage, and many tears, one of the mothers who visited our bereavement group shared her heart-wrenching account of what had happened to her son. She wept bitter tears about the death of her son who, just days before our meeting, had taken his own life. Being able to openly share what had happened must have lifted a tremendous weight off her shoulders that night. Her grief was so deep and fresh, it was difficult to know what to say.

Compassion flooded my heart as I cried with her, and as I saw the remorse and pain on her face. When she shared the details of her son's death, we all felt her pain, her heartache, and her grief; yet words would not suffice.

So we listened with our hearts, and at the end of the meeting, we all prayed for each other, and we prayed for her and her children.

This grieving mom had experienced the devastating loss of her precious son. For a parent, losing a child is one of the most overwhelming and painful experiences in life, but there are many other losses in life that may seem just as devastating to someone else. Loss of any kind brings with it an ending or separation, after which, things are forever different.

LOSS IS LOSS

Whether your loss is from the death of a loved one, the split-up of a family, the loss of a friendship, the loss of a job, a long-distance move, the loss of a favorite object, the loss of your home, or even the loss of a family pet—any type of loss (large or small) will create some degree of emotional trauma in your life.

Most of the emotional trauma and unwelcome challenges that come with loss involves dealing with your feelings and learning how to move on with your life, as shown in this next story. In his book, Recovering from the Losses of Life, author H. Norman Wright penned the following quote about a man who lost his job:

"When my company laid me off, I thought I would lose my mind. For years I had been successful in my business and had climbed higher and higher in my profession. Without my nameplate on my door, I felt stripped of everything. I felt I was nothing if I could not be the vice president. I coped very badly and in my devastation said some harmful things to my family."[1]

Everything in your life is different after loss. Whether you like it or not, the reality of your loss automatically sets in place a demarcation line—an ending of something that you once had and a beginning of something new. In addition to that, the wound of loss generates a landslide of complicated and mixed feelings and emotions called grief. The intensity of these feelings will depend on the intensity of your loss, which in turn, will determine the severity of your grief experience.

DEFINITION

How does one define this thing called grief? *Webster's Dictionary defines grief as "intense sorrow caused by the loss of a loved one, or deep mental anguish as that arising from bereavement"*[2] Grief can also be described as a sharp sorrow or painful regret due to any type of loss. Grief is how people feel as a result of loss. Sadness, anger, emptiness, depression, loneliness, guilt, despair, fear, denial, and hopelessness are a few of the many levels of despair and range of emotions that you will experience after a loss.

Contrary to popular belief, you are not losing your mind when you are grieving. The unpredictable and complicated emotional states you experience are all part of the mental process of coming to terms with loss.

Author Lorraine Peterson writes in her grief companion book entitled *Restore My Soul*, "Many of us experience a stunning mixture of emotional and spiritual states—from sadness to anger, from faith to despair. These moods move through us like weather fronts, so we find ourselves one moment placid, a short time later buffeted by an interior storm."[3]

Lorraine Peterson's devotional book on grief was an excellent tool that helped me identify and understand the many aspects about grief that were unfamiliar to me. What she wrote in her book really spoke to me, and the way she described what grief feels like was a comfort to read.

GET UNDERSTANDING

Gaining an understanding about your grief journey is important because understanding brings healing. Knowledge and understanding about what you can expect while grieving can help you better handle the painful process that follows a loss. Educating yourself about grief and loss will help you to prepare for all of the changes and mixed feelings that grief brings into your life. For example, your feelings may become so fragmented that you could easily go from crying one minute to laughing the next. Do not be alarmed when you experience a continuous stream of roller coaster or run away emotions. This is what grief is like.

If you know what to expect with grief, it can help you to embrace the process without the threat of getting stuck and possibly never getting past the pain of your loss. When you are stuck in grief, issues that stem from your loss are never resolved, and your recovery is almost always complicated and compromised. In some ways, your life will be on hold until these emotional issues are resolved.

Most people who are hurting do not understand that their emotional problems may lie in the fact that they have never fully grieved tragic loss and pain from their past.

RESPONSES VARY

Most people who have gone through a tragic loss would agree that the unwelcome changes and feelings that follow cannot be reduced to a neat list with absolutes on emotions, timelines, definitions, goals, or completion dates. Because each individual is unique, the process of grief is a very personal journey. Everyone's grief timeline is different. And the grief journey itself looks different on each person. Your response can be affected by a number of things such as personality, family, coping skills, age, culture, maturity level, gender, and spiritual beliefs. In some cases, even the manner of death or circumstances surrounding your loss can affect your response.

Getting beyond grief takes understanding, time, prayer, participation, education, and most of all, lots of work. You can expedite the healing process if you choose to do the work. This means that you must find constructive and healing ways to cope with your loss. It also means that you do not suppress your feelings, but learn how to express them in healthy ways that will benefit your recovery. Otherwise, unresolved feelings of grief will remain with you, only causing more problems down the road.

WAYS OF COPING

The key is to do what works best for you. Find something positive and healthy to do that brings comfort, peace, and encouragement into your life. My father found a great way to remember Stephanie by planting a garden in her memory. He and my mother took some of the green plants that were left from Stephanie's funeral, and along with planting a few other flowers, made a beautiful garden situated not far from their outdoor patio. My parents even put a picture of Stephanie in the garden.

Just walking by and looking at this simple, little patch of green plants and colorful flowers that my father labored over in love, kept a part of Stephanie alive in our hearts. His idea had provided a unique outlet for our family to grieve.

Whenever anyone visited, my father would always bring them to see his garden.

The following is a suggested list of things you can do to better cope with everyday living while in the process of recovery:

- **Pray**—Spend time talking and listening to God and find healing scriptures in the Bible to pray over yourself.
- **Receive personal prayer ministry**—Receive prayer for specific areas of emotional hurt from a licensed minister.
- **Journal**—Write out your thoughts and feelings on paper.
- **Reach out to others**—Help someone else with a need in their life; help with outreach at church or through a community organization.
- **Take time for recreation or outdoor activities**—Have fun by going to the movies, looking at pictures of your loved ones, or listening to music. Watching a sunset, taking walks along the beach, or playing sports are good outlets as well.
- **Read grief material**—Read and glean from books and articles about grief recovery, or any other inspiring subject you might enjoy.
- **Spend time with family and friends**—Enjoy fellowship and intimacy with friends and family. Be open to making new friends during this time.

- **Worship**—Sing songs of love and adoration from your heart to God while in church or during your personal prayer time.
- **Schedule quiet times of rest**—Get enough physical rest or sit restfully before God soaking in His presence. Taking quiet times of reflection while thinking about your deceased loved one is a good way to remember them and is good therapy for you.
- **See a grief counselor or therapist**—Seek professional help and guidance.
- **Take time just for you**—If you are a woman, do things that make you feel good about yourself—get a new hairdo, get a pedicure or manicure, go to the spa, or go shopping. Likewise, for men—get new clothes, get a haircut, join a health club, go hunting or fishing, or buy some new gadget that keeps you occupied.
- **Join a support group**—Get support from others who have already gone through your type of loss.
- **Enjoy a hobby or work on a special project**—Do whatever you may enjoy doing: painting, drawing, crocheting, or scrap booking, are a few ideas.
- **Learn a new skill**—Take a class in your community offered by a professional, or register for a class offered by your local community college.
- **Vacation with family or friends**—Go somewhere you have always wanted to go, such as on a cruise or to another country.

- **Write a good-bye letter**—This is a healing way to say good-bye to your loss and to express your feelings, thoughts, and emotions about it on paper.
- **Laugh**—Laugh often with family and friends, and sometimes even with strangers. Watch a funny movie that will make you laugh or spend time with someone who has a great sense of humor.

The main idea is to get involved in whatever activities that appeal to you. If nothing comes to mind, pray and ask God to reveal a specific activity that would benefit you while you are grieving. Be willing to try new things. Being able to deal with everyday life requires doing whatever helpful thing you can do to get better, and to move beyond your present pain.

Put one foot in front of the other each and every day until you cross the finish line of grief.

ACTION PLAN

From the onset of your loss, develop a strategy or plan of action for grieving. The first thing would be to pray and ask God to give you a strategy for your recovery and wisdom for the road ahead of you. One suggestion is to learn as much as you can about grief, and then implement whatever positive action plan that works best for your lifestyle. Remember that your grief journey continues whether you choose to participate in the process or not.

JOURNALING

One positive exercise that helped me through the process of grief was journaling. Journaling is keeping a record of your thoughts and feelings on paper. There was something very therapeutic about releasing what was in my heart and in my head onto a piece of paper. Writing helps you sort through and get in touch with your feelings and emotions.

The following thoughts about grief were taken from my personal journal:

> No one can go to school to learn how to grieve. I guess there is no right or wrong way. Everyone's pain is individual. Each person handles the beast within in a different way. Grief is a feeling on the inside that transcends the mind, terrorizes the soul, and tears apart the heart.
>
> Grief is a feeling that makes you think that you are losing your bearings, your life has been turned upside down, and nothing seems right anymore. You have no realities, nothing to hold on to—nowhere to go for relief. Grieving occurs when something has been taken away from you without an explanation, an apology, or a promise of return. You are left feeling vulnerable and weak.
>
> You wonder how you can ever plan to have something precious in your life when, at any time, it could be taken from you, knowing that if one other

precious thing were taken from you that it would be the final blow against your life. Satan wants to make that final blow against God's people—only God can keep it from happening.

At the time that I penned these thoughts about grief, the shock and numbness of losing my daughter had worn off and I was beginning to feel the full weight and impact of her death. Looking back on this time in my life, I was totally clueless about grief. Having some knowledge about grief would have benefited me greatly in the beginning of my journey. At the least, I would have understood what grief was all about and have had some idea of how to deal with the painful emotions that followed.

EMBRACE THE PROCESS

Even though I was good at journaling, I was not good at grieving. It would be several years after my daughter's death before I began to grieve. Not until a friend of mine made the comment that I had never grieved the loss of my daughter did I give it much thought. He was right though; I had not allowed myself to grieve.

I had been so consumed with ministry and trying to keep my life afloat on a daily basis that I had not taken the time to work toward my own recovery. I had suppressed my feelings because I thought expressing them might be viewed as a sign of weakness. In doing so, I had put undue pressure and stress upon myself to tough it out.

PERMISSION TO GRIEVE

I had not given myself permission to grieve – to process it – to feel it – to let it run its course through me. As a Christian, I thought that I had to endure the pain and never complain. Otherwise, it would be considered a lack of faith or a bad witness for Christ. Misconceptions or legalistic thinking about grief can keep you from the healing and freedom that is yours in Christ Jesus.

Author Victor M. Parachin writes about one woman's introduction to grief in his book, *Grief Relief*: "Four years after her husband died, a widow said that it would have been great comfort and help to her to have been informed of what grief would entail. She said:

> If only someone whom I respected had sat me down after Martin died and said, "Now, Lynn, bereavement is a wound. It's like being very, very badly hurt. You will grieve and that is painful. And your grief will have many stages, but all of them will be healing. Little by little, you will be whole again. And you will be a stronger person. Just as a broken bone knits and becomes stronger than before, so will you."[4]

Like the widow you just read about, knowing what grief entails will help you better understand your journey, or at the least, help you avoid getting stuck in the process. Knowing what to expect will help eliminate the fears that many people have about grieving. Even though I struggled with the emotional side of grief for a long time, God in His great mercy and love, arranged a time and season for me to finish grieving and to put closure on my past.

Psalm 31:14-15 (NIV) states, "But I trust in you, O LORD; I say, 'You are my God'. My times are in your hands."

I learned that if I did not embrace the tools necessary to help me assimilate my loss and move beyond the pain I was feeling, I would never heal. Once you embrace the process, though, you can begin to make real progress in your grief journey.

And as time goes on, your progress will produce the final product of healing. It sounds like a formula but it is far from being a formula.

Each individual griever must be willing to take the knowledge and the resources available, along with God's help, and incorporate them into their daily lives.

No one can do that for you.

THE PURPOSE OF GRIEF

Experiencing a tragic loss does not have to destroy your life or cause you to become a bitter person. If you are willing to embrace your grief journey, there are tremendous benefits that this process can produce within you:

- You can choose to move beyond grief into a place of healing.
- You can use your experience to become a better person.
- You can grow spiritually as a result of your experience.
- You can take your pain and turn it into a platform to help someone else, just as Candy Lightner did when her daughter was killed.

In her article entitled, "25 Years of Saving Lives," freelance journalist, Laurie Davies wrote this about Candy: "Twenty-five years ago, a heartbroken mother made a pledge in her deceased daughter's bedroom. She would do something about the outrage of drunk driving—a decision that quickly inspired a handful of grieving, determined mothers to join in the fight."[5] Candy Lightner founded an organization called MADD (Mothers Against Drunk Driving) that is now helping victims of crime across the nation.

Your pain has purpose and can be turned into a platform to help others.

CHANGE AND TRANSITION

The pain and process of loss automatically throws you into a cycle of change and transition. Change comes whether you welcome it or not, but you can choose how you handle the changes you are faced with, and whether or not you will grow through your experiences. ***Remember that change is inevitable but growth is optional.***

Moving into a new home was one of the first major changes I made after losing my daughter. Every time I passed by her bedroom, I relived the events of her death. Because of that, a new setting became vital to my recovery.

Another positive change I made was going back to college to complete my undergraduate degree. The timing of going back to school proved to be a good project to keep me busy. College gave me a new focus and healthy diversion from the familiar. It challenged me intellectually and forced me to socialize and interact with others.

DECISION MAKING

Change can be a positive thing, but exercise caution when making big decisions that will affect you and your family for years to come. A good rule to follow is to avoid making any drastic changes or decisions when you are emotionally distraught.

This is a prime time that most people may not be thinking clearly.

Many of the decisions you make while you are hurting or in the middle of a crisis would be quite different if made from a healed position when things have settled down and you are clear-headed again.

When people are in crisis, there seems to be a knee jerk reaction to "do something" in an effort to fix a problem or make it go away altogether. This is unrealistic thinking because grief will not go away until it is processed. You may be able to suppress your grief, but you will never be able to overcome it unless you are willing to do the grief work required.

My advice is that you pray over every decision you make, in addition to seeking godly counsel for any major life changes you might be considering.

Proverbs 11:14 states that, "... in the multitude of counselors there is safety."

WORKING WOUNDED

After Stephanie passed away, I threw myself completely into my work. Those who knew me had always accused me of being "addicted" to the ministry; and they were right. I loved the work of the ministry; I loved serving and leading; I loved the challenge of it all and seeing the results of changed lives.

Close friends and relatives advised me to take an extended leave of absence from ministry. That idea seemed to be the right thing to do, but after praying about it, and discussing it with my pastor, I decided that it would be better in the long run for me to keep working.

As it turned out, the discipline and routine of working every day was a wise decision. Keeping a daily work schedule, coupled with the many interactions I had with other people on staff, in meetings, and in other settings was an important key to my recovery.

Staying busy helped me to manage the "emotional weather fronts" that come as randomly and as unpredictably as Texas weather. One helpful hint to managing your grief is to be able to discern for yourself when it is time to press on and when you should step back for a time of rest and recuperation.

But keep in mind that if you take time out to recuperate but fail to reinvest in the grief process, it can be just as harmful as pressuring yourself to do too much, too soon.

One factor that gave me courage to keep pressing on was the responsibility I felt toward those who had listened to my counsel over the years. My advice to others in crisis was always, "Come on, you can do it! Don't give up! God will make a way; you just have to trust Him!" Now it was time to take my own counsel and practice what I preached.

What I expected of others, I could do no less myself.

ONE DAY AT A TIME

Regardless of how much I tried to *tough it out*, there were still days when the pain of losing my daughter became all-consuming. However, on those days I would find myself being uplifted in a variety of ways:

- By talking with someone and through a conversation be encouraged,

- God would highlight a specific scripture in my prayer time that really spoke to me,
- I would attend a faith building church service,
- God would use me in someone else's life,
- I would read something inspiring in a book,
- I would simply wake up the next morning feeling much better about everything. On days like that, I knew someone had been praying for me. The Bible says that Jesus ever lives to intercede for you. (See Hebrews 7:25.)

God used the very people that I had helped in the past to be a continual source of encouragement and support to me during my recovery period. Unfortunately, there is no easy fix or magic wand to wave when it comes to overcoming grief and loss. In retrospect, it was the culmination of all of these things that I have shared that made a significant difference in living everyday life. And God used all of it to keep me moving forward in the healing process.

REACHING OUT TO OTHERS

As I continued to reach out to others, I was able to look beyond my own problems, and to stop feeling sorry for myself. Whatever good thing you do for others, the Lord will reward you with the same. The principle of sowing and reaping means that what you give out, you will receive back in return. As I was giving out of my own need, I was not only blessing others, but I was being helped myself. ***Reaching out to others will be an important key to your recovery because Ephesians 6:8 promises, "Knowing that whatsoever good thing any man doeth, the same shall he receive of the Lord, whether he be bond or free."***

KEEP MINISTERING

Every week, the church outreach group that I directed went into the inner city to help families in need. We prayed with people, listened to their life stories, handed out food, taught Sunday school to the children, and shared our faith. In the course of time, we started an inner city ministry to at-risk families—we also started a bus ministry, sidewalk Sunday school ministry, helping hands ministry, visitation ministry, homeless ministry, and Superchurch children's ministry.

Having something to commit to on a regular basis afforded me a ministry outlet and something to look forward to each week. You may not want to do exactly what I did, but the point here is that you put your hands to something. God will bless the works of your hands and you will feel much better about yourself as you give out of your own need.

Thousands of people were led to the Lord during that time. God used my work in church ministry to be a continual source of inspiration to me. Even in the midst of your pain, God can still use you to help others, if you let Him. Remember that God still uses wounded soldiers!

GIVING OUT

In the New Testament, Jesus commended the widow who gave two mites as an offering because she had given all that she had. He explained that her sacrifice was even greater than someone who had given from his or her abundance because when she gave, she gave out of her need. (See Mark 12:43-44.)

God is greatly moved when you give out of your need because it then becomes a living sacrifice that is acceptable and pleasing in His sight.

In addition to giving out of your need, another principle to remember is to plant a seed when you have a need. The key is to give something freely that can be sown to reap a harvest. (You could sow an offering, give a gift to someone, help someone else who has a need, make something for someone, cook a meal for someone, visit a shut-in, etc.) No matter what your circumstances are, giving in faith will always move the hand of God on your behalf.

Going out each week for outreach ministry allowed me the opportunity to not only plant a seed, but to give out of my need. It also kept me from isolating myself and retreating from the rest of the world. As I helped those families in need, I was really reaping the greater benefit.

Reaching out to them helped me feel better about my own situation and less focused on myself.

BEING THANKFUL

Having a heart of thankfulness is an important aspect of your grief journey. God wants you to genuinely choose to give thanks from your heart no matter what circumstances you are facing. Therefore, reaching a place where you can truly be thankful in all things is vital to your recovery.

1 Thessalonians 5:18 says, "In every thing give thanks: for this is the will of God in Christ Jesus concerning you."

God is not asking you to be thankful for your loss, but in the midst of loss, disappointment, and pain He wants you to keep an attitude of gratitude.

The key to being thankful in all things is to understand that everything in your life is a gift from God, and ultimately belongs to Him. *Whatever you have lost in life initially came to you as a gift and blessing from God—even if you had to work to get it—it was still a gift from God.* It was placed in your hands to care for, steward over, and simply enjoy. Everything you have—your children, family, friends, job, and your money—all came from the generous hands of God.

It was difficult at first to view the loss of my daughter in this light, but I had to remember that God had given Stephanie (and all of my children) to our family as a gift.

Instead of focusing on the fact that she was gone, I needed to see the good that came out of the life Stephanie lived, and our times spent together, and focus on those higher thoughts.

I was thankful for those last years we had together before her death, realizing that they were a precious gift that only God could have given.

The Bible says to give thanks *in* all things, not *for* all things. **This does not mean that you give thanks for your loss, but it means that you are to remain thankful in spite of what you have lost. This is the heart attitude that God blesses.** Being thankful is a matter of the heart, stemming from a positive mental attitude that continues to believe in the goodness and trustworthiness of God.

The key to keeping a thankful heart is to look for the silver lining in everything, look for the good in others, rely on the faithfulness of God, keep giving, and remember the many blessings you still enjoy in this life.

MAKING ADJUSTMENTS

Give yourself permission to make whatever adjustments or changes are necessary to help you cope with everyday living. Most people understand themselves well enough to know what will or will not work for them.

Do not feel guilty about making adjustments, and do not allow previous obligations to force you into uncomfortable situations. Sometimes you have to opt out of an event or special celebration that may cause you to become too emotional.

Your ability to handle perfectly normal social settings may be a challenge, and you may struggle more with your emotions during the holidays.

Accept the fact that it may be difficult or awkward to celebrate and rejoice with others for their special occasions such as social events, weddings, holiday parties, or baby showers.

For me, Christmas functions are still challenging because they always remind me of my last Christmas party with my daughter. You may have a similar struggle; therefore, do what works best for you and your family.

Attending funerals may be out of the question for you in the beginning, and most people would understand completely if you had to "bow out gracefully."

EXPECT SETBACKS

Every now and then you may have a setback, so go ahead and pre-approve them. At first, setbacks may occur on a regular basis, but eventually they will become more sporadic and should dissipate altogether in time. Experiencing a setback is like taking two giant steps forward and twenty giant steps backwards.

Your wide range of emotions and ever changing behavior will eventually level out. Sometimes, the setbacks come when you least expect them and in the most inopportune places.

I was in church one Easter Sunday (about one year after Stephanie passed away) when such a setback occurred. My pastor was teaching on how Jesus raised Jairus' daughter from the dead. I started crying and could not stop. I had to leave the service to compose myself. While the pastor was preaching, all I could think of was the fact that I had been a faith failure.

I had worked so hard at suppressing this "ungodly belief" until it surfaced that day, wanting me to accept it as truth. An ungodly belief is any belief that does not agree with the Word of God. That little nagging voice on the inside that constantly accused me of not having enough faith was just too much to handle.

Overwhelmed by what I was feeling, I abruptly ran out of the service that morning. When asked what was wrong, all I could do was cry, and cry, and cry. A friend tried to console me but I did not want to be consoled. I needed to cry, to let go of my bottled up pain, frustration, and fear. Afterwards, I noticed that I felt better. Crying had actually helped me.

How can you gauge if crying is healthy or not? Healthy crying is crying that leads to an emotional release that is actually freeing, opposed to crying that leads to more depression and emotional pain. How you feel after you cry will determine if the experience was healthy or unhealthy.

Do not feel weak or embarrassed about crying. Although they may have heard all their lives that real men don't cry, men need to cry sometimes. In all of his glory and power, even Jesus cried and grieved at the tomb of his friend Lazarus.

Crying is one of the ways you grieve and you heal.

CRYING IS GOOD

The book entitled *Grief Relief* had this to say about crying: "... researchers are verifying that crying is good for us because tears reduce tensions, remove dangerous toxins, and increase the body's ability to heal itself."[6]

Crying helps to release the emotional pain you have bottled up on the inside. These intermittent and sometimes unexpected bouts of crying may keep you from totally internalizing your pain, or prevent a future emotional explosion or breakdown.

Crying has a way of saying, "*I acknowledge my pain and loss.*"

The Lord showed me that crying was like pulling the scab off a wound and letting the pus or infection ooze out. Just like a physical wound—once the pus is drained, it will begin to dry up and heal. Likewise, once the pus of emotional pain is drained and released, further healing can take place.

With this in mind, do not feel bad. Please, go ahead and cry!

FAITH FAILURE?

As I listened to the teaching that day in church and compared it to my own experience, I thought I had failed. I had believed God for Stephanie's physical healing, and it had not happened. I could no longer ignore the question—*Was her death a faith failure on my part?*

The answer was *No*.

Please do not allow Satan to torment you with this "faith failure" lie. Your loss was not a faith failure and you are not a failure. Romans 8:37 decrees that we are "...more than conquerors through him that loved us."

Being more than a conqueror is the complete opposite of being a failure. When your circumstances point to failure, you must place your faith in the unseen realm where God resides. 2 Corinthians 4:17-18 states,

> For our light affliction, which is but for a moment, worketh for us a far more exceeding and eternal weight of glory; while we look not at the things which are seen, but at the things which are not seen: for the things which are seen are temporal; but the things which are not seen are eternal.

Give God time to work things out for your good, because what God works for your good is where your victory lies and where your testimony begins. I knew that if I was ever going to heal from the loss of my daughter, then it was time to believe the truth of God's Word for my life. This meant that no matter how I felt about my loss, or how badly I was hurting, it was time to trust God with it all.

TRIGGER POINTS

You may get emotional over some of the simplest things, or something may catch you off guard that triggers a painful memory. While I was still freshly grieving, when I saw or heard anything that reminded me of Stephanie, my immediate response was one of deep sadness—sometimes even anger. One day while out shopping, I noticed a lady who was around Stephanie's height and build. She had long black hair like my daughter's, and she was wearing a gray suit.

Stephanie had a certain style of dressing, and one of her favorite colors was gray. There was one gray jacket in particular that she wore all the time. This stranger's resemblance to my daughter was uncanny. My heart sank for a moment. My emotions all rushed to the scene. Obviously, it was not my daughter. I took a deep breath, regained my composure, and walked away with a knot in my throat.

When something triggers a memory of your loss and you are tempted to become emotional, the best thing to do is just shake it off. Learn to recognize your trigger points and be prepared to reel yourself in before you spiral out of control emotionally. The key to handling your trigger points is to allow yourself to feel your feelings but be sure to maintain your composure at the same time.

Once the Lord began to heal me, however, those painful emotions that tried to arise were not as intense as before. Whenever I saw something that reminded me of my daughter, pleasant memories came to mind instead of painful ones.

This was one way I was able to gauge how well I was doing and how far I had come. You just handle things better. You recognize the emotional traps that cause you to revisit your pain. You stop overreacting to insignificant things that will not matter in the larger scope of eternity.

MOMENTS COME AND MOMENTS GO

In early grief, heightened and wounded emotions may cause you to feel sad, or they may cause you to withdraw altogether from others. When this happens, you may be experiencing a "moment." Moments are times when something (anything) triggers your emotions, causing you to revisit your pain and revisit your loss as if it happened just yesterday.

Moments make you feel like the bottom has fallen out of your world, and in your mind you are at the gravesite of your loss, experiencing firsthand every emotion and heartache you felt when it first happened. Your heart breaks again. Nothing matters anymore. Everything becomes surreal. Time stops.

Moments can become so emotionally draining that you may not be able to function as usual. ***Remember that it is okay to have moments—just do not let the moments have you.*** Your life cannot be controlled by your moments, but sometimes a mental time-out is just what you need.

When I experienced those moments, I found that if I would discipline myself to spend time with God, and at the same time begin to journal what was going on inside of me, it helped to release the intense emotions that I was feeling, and it helped me to get everything back into perspective.

The following is a guide that will help you process your moments back into reality:

- Talk to someone who is confidential, discreet and compassionate, and someone who is a good listener about what you are feeling.
- Pray about the situation at the onset. Do not allow your emotions to worsen or escalate before taking time out to pray.
- Spend quality time with God just sitting in His presence and meditating on His great love for you. Playing soft worship music at the same time can be very soothing and comforting.
- Journal about thoughts and feelings that triggered your moment.
- If needed, take time away from your normal activities to pray, regroup, and refocus.
- Do not make any quick, rash decisions when you are having a moment.
- If nothing else is working, pamper yourself out of your moment. (Review the list of ideas in this chapter.)

Allow yourself to have your moments, take a deep breath, and then move on to regain the ground you lost. The intense feelings that brought on the moments will eventually level out, and as time goes on, you will learn how to handle your emotions better.

CHILDREN IN GRIEF

Each person's response to grief will vary. Your response usually depends upon your relationship to the deceased. For example, my children Richard and Candace responded differently to Stephanie's death than I did. This is not to diminish their pain or their love for Stephanie, but studies suggest that parents who lose children experience a much deeper sense of loss than do siblings. Because of this, it may take parents longer to heal.

Children will also grieve differently than adults. Their reaction to loss is based on their age, maturity level, and relationship to the deceased. When an entire family is grieving, children may be innocently overlooked or their emotional needs neglected before anyone realizes what is happening.

Family members should be encouraged and reminded to spend as much time as possible with the grieving child or adolescent, allowing them time to talk and express their feelings and work through their grief emotions. Studies indicate that children may even feel guilty or responsible for a loved one's death. They should have someone in their lives that can reassure them and help them work through their feelings of guilt.

Unfortunately, children are sometimes left all alone to find answers to their questions and to try to understand why they feel the way they do. Parents should try as much as possible to be sensitive to their child's spiritual and emotional needs during this time. If the child's grief continues over a prolonged period of time, seeking professional help or therapy is advised.

WRITE A GOODBYE LETTER

The most painful grief, however, is when you lose someone and there were unresolved issues and conflicts left in the relationship. Perhaps you were at odds or not speaking to the deceased person before he or she died. Maybe there were no conflicts in your relationship but you never had a chance to say goodbye. Grief survivors in these situations may never finish grieving because they feel that there can never be reconciliation or proper closure with their loss.

Something that may help to bring closure to your loss is for you to take the time to write a letter of reconciliation or a goodbye letter to your deceased loved one or to the loss (job, pet, etc.) you have suffered. Writing a letter allows you to express from your heart what you were not able to say, or did not have the opportunity to say before the loss occurred.

Once you have written the letter, you can tear it up or keep it for as long as you wish. The letter is for your eyes only and for your benefit, unless you choose to share it with others. Writing a letter of reconciliation or a goodbye letter allows you to express your feelings, and in doing so, make peace with and bring closure to your loss. Not only will it help to bring closure but it will also bring healing and comfort to your heart.

TALKING ABOUT IT

Talking about your loss is a therapeutic way to process your grief. There were times that I wanted to talk about the details of Stephanie's death, and then there were periods that I wanted to reminisce about special times and fond memories of us together. At other times, I wanted to be alone in order to think, to sort through things, and to be still before the Lord. As mentioned earlier, having a good listener to share your thoughts and feelings with is therapeutic and will help you to heal faster.

MEN IN GRIEF

Because of personality and gender differences, men and women do not grieve the same way. Keep in mind, though, that there is no right or wrong way to grieve. Men may throw themselves into their work or other recreational outlets that may help them better cope with their loss. However, men sometimes have more of a tendency to cocoon themselves or shut themselves off from others; therefore, they should be careful to guard against this type of unhealthy response.

They may not want to dialogue about their pain, where women may find greater comfort and release in talking about their loss. Studies show that women speak about 20,000 words per day while men speak an average of 7000 words per day. Women may need to talk, and talk, and talk. Someone should be there to listen.

Men are often called silent grievers. They may not want to talk as much as women, but someone should be there to understand and support them, as they are grieving in their own unique way.

These are a few suggestions that can help men through the process of grief:

- Be open and talk about how you feel with others.
- Take time to grieve over your loss.
- Learn how to communicate and not just isolate.
- Keep your relationships with family and friends a priority.
- Find healthy outlets and activities outside of your work.

Whether you are male or female, child or adult, you should stay open to the help and support others may want to give you. Helping you may be just the therapy they need as well, as giving of yourself always has a reciprocal benefit.

HELPING A FRIEND WITH GRIEF

Suffering alone will only amplify your pain; therefore, it is important to have a good support system of friends and relatives available to you throughout your grief journey. After Stephanie died, my church family surrounded me with continuous love and support. Whatever I needed, they were there to help me. I credit much of my progress during that time to their account.

Recognize your need for others during this time. Welcome family and friends, or whomever God sends your way. You may need emotional support, financial support, or you may need practical help with your day-to-day obligations. For example, something as simple as having someone to clean your home, take the trash out, or go to the grocery store for you can be a huge relief.

Perhaps just having another person in your home that will sit and visit with you would be helpful. As stated previously, a good listener is always therapeutic, since processing grief includes talking things out, sometimes even rambling.

Simple activities that you accomplished before your loss without a second thought may overwhelm you for now. Allow others to fill in the gaps and help with these simple everyday tasks. People want to show their love and support by being able to help you with something, even the smallest things.

God has handpicked those who are willing to help you bear this burden. You do not have to go through this time of grieving alone. The key is to recognize and be willing to accept a hand extended in your direction because God will send the most wonderful people across your path.

Their love will help buffer the deep hurt and void that you feel. ***Understand that your relationship with others who accept and support you will be a vital link to your recovery.*** In the book, God Will Make a Way, authors Drs. Henry Cloud and John Townsend shed light on this subject. "People can also learn to be afraid of intimacy if they have been hurt, betrayed, abandoned, or rejected by people who they trusted. Remember, you were made for relationship. If you are dealing with fears, you need other people. Support and love drive fear away."[7]

SPECIAL FRIENDS

I asked one of my longtime friends, Brenda, who was a tremendous help to me after my daughter passed away, to share some of her thoughts about helping a friend who is grieving. This is what she had to say:

When trying to comfort or help someone who is grieving, the best thing you can do is to just be there for them. The tendency with most people who want to help is to try to "fix" something. But you must realize that you cannot fix anything. And sometimes you cannot say anything that will make it better. The grieving person has just experienced the most devastating, critical injury to their soul that anyone could ever possibly receive. Sometimes a quick fix, or mere words, would simply be like trying to place a little band-aid on a severe, open wound.

What the grieving person needs more than anything is for you just to be there with them. Sometimes, even conversation is not needed; they just need to know that you are there. The grieving person is experiencing agonizing inner pain and may at times seem upset with you, at other times they may seem indifferent, act out of character, or any number of surprising actions and reactions. But you must remember that their unpredictable behavior is not to be taken personally. You must be mature enough to recognize this and still keep hanging in there with them. Stay in the relationship because they need you more than they know it at the time.

They may need assistance with simple, everyday things like returning phone calls, running errands, sending cards, paying bills, cleaning the house, etc. You may need to take them on short excursions just to get them out of the house for a little while.

But again, the most important thing you can do is just being there—for a week, a month, a year, or more if necessary. Whatever time it takes to allow them the time and space for their critical wounds to heal.

It is also a great help and comfort when you remember all of the special anniversaries (birthday, anniversary, date of death, etc) of their deceased loved one. I almost always do one or all of the following: call on the phone, send a card, or send flowers. This lets the grieving person know that you remember their loss, that you are sharing in their pain, and that they are not going through it alone.

Be sensitive to them when they need to talk, when they just need a quiet companion, or when they need to get out of the house. Learn to be sensitive to their "trigger points" and to their "moments" as explained in this chapter. And most importantly, never rush them, push them, or try to hurry them through the process of grieving; yet at the same time, speak words of faith and encourage them to believe God for their total and complete healing."

FAMILIES IN GRIEF

Grief emotions may go up and down like a roller coaster at times, and in addition, your responses to people, situations, and circumstances may fluctuate from day to day. During your grieving period, relatives and friends must be advised not to take anything personally, and to not allow themselves to get caught in the loop of your emotional highs and lows.

If you are going to make progress in your grief journey, remember the other people in your life who still need you to be strong for them. Each family member is dealing with their own pain independently and sometimes privately, but you still need to stay conscious of others affected by the loss.

Staying conscious means that you make a deliberate effort to participate and embrace the recovery process—for the good of yourself and everyone else.

Friends would sometimes tell me, "You're stronger than you think you are." Most people are usually stronger than they give themselves credit for. Somehow tragedy has a way of drawing out of people an inner strength and fortitude they did not know existed. But sometimes tragedy will bring out the worst in a person or family, causing greater division in the lives of those who are already grieving and hurting.

When this happens, it is not the heart of God, for He desires that anything you face in life would produce within you greater humility, greater love, and greater compassion for each other. God wants you to have an even greater value for the preciousness of each life.

Because the grief process is different for every person, families should respect each other's personal journey with grief and become more intentional about staying in harmony with one another.

If families were at odds with each other before the loss, the trauma could make things worse; but on the other hand, it could bring everyone together in a time of reconciliation. God has given each believer the ministry of reconciliation (2 Corinthians 5:18). You are not exempt from this ministry because of a suffered loss.

Praying for the individual who is grieving, and allowing them the space they need, is a wonderful gift that others can give someone who is desperately hurting from a tragic loss. You will never be able to fully understand what a person is going through, but try to put yourself in that person's shoes and treat them the way you would want to be treated.

Matthew 7:12 (NKJV), [the Golden Rule] states, "Therefore, whatever you want men to do to you, do also to them, for this is the Law and the Prophets."

When an entire family unit is grieving, it may be difficult for each member of that family to be there for the other person, or to completely understand what the other person is going through. Though you may all be in the same family, each of you will process grief differently. You must remember that the other person's thoughts, feelings, and their way of dealing with things may be completely different than yours. However, it does not diminish the gravity of their grief.

As stated earlier, remember that children are affected by loss, and need help dealing with and understanding their feelings, just as adults need help. Try to develop a strategy for your family's grief journey that factors in everyone concerned.

My son Richard matured to another level after his sister's death. I saw bravery and inner strength in him that I had not seen before. He was a major support to his father during that difficult time, and it brought both of them much closer together. Both of my children dealt with the loss of their sister with strength of character, resilience, and great inner fortitude.

Whether you are a parent, mate, child, relative, friend, co-worker, or casual acquaintance, try to remain as understanding and sensitive as possible to all who have been affected by the tragedy.

Give them enough time and space to grieve in their own unique way, but the bottom line for everyone is to understand the importance of grieving, because only grieving will lead to healing.

SUMMING IT UP

There are no quick remedies for overcoming grief—you cannot just will yourself out of it—you cannot go around it—you must go through it.

There are some things in life you have to go through in order to get through.

Embracing the process means that you will do the grief work required, and that you are committed to seeing the process through until your recovery is complete. Even though other people can help you, there are some things in the grief process that only you can accomplish. The process takes time; so let time be your friend. In time, you will notice that you have made some progress. You may not be where you want to be, but you will be much further along than where you were. Remember to celebrate each milestone you make in your healing journey.

A grieving person is able to integrate back into the mainstream of life when they do not allow themselves to wallow in grief for an indefinite amount of time. Give yourself enough time to grieve, but pray for God to heal your wounded heart. Jesus came to heal you spirit, soul, and body as stated in Isaiah 53:3-5:

>...He is despised and rejected of men; a man of sorrows, and acquainted with grief: and we hid as it were our faces from him; he was despised, and we esteemed him not. Surely he hath borne our griefs,

and carried our sorrows: yet we did esteem him stricken, smitten of God, and afflicted. But he was wounded for our transgressions, he was bruised for our iniquities: the chastisement of our peace was upon him; and with his stripes we are healed.

Healing belongs to you. Complete your grief work and believe God to complete your healing!

Processing Grief Prayer

Dear Heavenly Father,

I come before you in the name of Jesus. I ask you to help me with the pain I am feeling because of losing _____.

Please help me to see things through your eyes, and help me to keep a grateful heart in spite of everything that has happened.

I decree that I am strong in you and in the power of Your might (Ephesians 6:10).

Holy Spirit, help me to grieve and mourn according to God's Word. Your Word says that "Blessed are they that mourn: for they shall be comforted" (Matthew 5:4). I receive your comfort now.

I receive your grace and I confess that your grace is sufficient for me; and in my weakness your strength is made perfect. (1 Corinthians 12:9)

I confess that I can do all things through Christ who strengthens me. (Philippians 4:13) I confess that no weapon formed against me shall prosper. (Isaiah 54:17) I confess that I always triumph in Christ Jesus. (1 Corinthians 2:14)

Lord, I ask you to heal me from this pain and make me whole again. I receive my healing now, in Jesus name. Amen.

JOURNAL NOTES

Chapter Four

UNDERSTANDING GRIEF EMOTIONS

> *In the multitude of my [anxious] thoughts within me, Your comforts cheer and delight my soul! Psalm 94:19 (AMP)*

The biggest dilemma in processing grief is dealing with the multitude of negative emotions that seem to come out of nowhere and hit your mind at lightening speed. One of the first things that a friend said to me after my daughter's death was, "Do not condemn yourself, and do not let the devil condemn you. You were a good mother. Always remember that you were a good mother." The Holy Spirit would gently remind me of these timely words of encouragement whenever I began to think that it was my fault Stephanie had died.

CONDEMNATION

Condemnation is a problem for many people, especially those who have suffered loss. *Webster's Dictionary* defines *condemnation* as: "*...to declare to be wrong, to convict of guilt, to sentence judicially, and to pronounce unfit for use.*"[1] When you condemn yourself, you essentially become your own judge and jury and pronounce yourself guilty as charged. When you do this, you alone have brought a charge against yourself; no one else has condemned you.

How do you know when you are condemning yourself? When you begin to believe the lie that you are unfit and unworthy, and the negative emotions and what you believe about yourself become your own personal truth. When you feel the need to be punished and nothing you do is ever enough to satisfy the penalty you have pronounced against yourself. As mentioned in the previous chapter, these thought processes and judgments fall into a category of ungodly beliefs.

Personal tragedies should never validate beliefs that are contrary to the Word of God. The pain of loss and intense grief emotions may cause even the most spiritually mature person to accept a belief or thought that is not of God. Authors and ministers, Chester and Betsy Kylstra, in their book *Restoring the Foundations,* define ungodly beliefs as "lies about ourselves, about others, and about God, and they are dangerous because they affect our perceptions, our decisions, and our actions."[2]

One example of ungodly beliefs is the things that people will allow themselves to believe in trying to come to terms with their loss. I once heard an individual tell a crowd of people that his child had died because God needed another flower in Heaven. I am sure that the thought of his child being another flower in Heaven brought great comfort to him. However, this statement was not scriptural, and therefore untrue.

The Bible says in Proverbs 23:7 that, ". . . as he thinketh in his heart, so is he." You are the sum total of who you think you are. If you think you are wrong, faulty, or guilty (even if you are not), you will act on what you think and not on what you believe.

RECOGNIZE WRONG THOUGHTS

Recognizing thoughts of condemnation (ungodly beliefs) is not always as obvious as could be expected. *You may not verbalize what you believe, but you punish yourself inwardly by entertaining accusing thoughts about assumed shortcomings, failures, or mistakes from your past.* Entertaining these thoughts will eventually manifest in outward negative behaviors, with the potential to swing as far and wide as suicidal thinking.

One example that comes to mind is a situation that happened to someone whom I never suspected was struggling with self-hate and thoughts of suicide. She is the most loving and caring person I know. She was struggling, however, with feelings of condemnation and inward hatred toward herself over an assumed failure from her past.

Her self-hate became so intense that one day she looked in the mirror and slapped her face as hard as she could out of sheer frustration and contempt that she had for herself. This individual blamed herself for her failed marriage.

By slapping her face, she was telling herself, "I hate you, and you need to be punished. So, I am going to be the one to do it." She struggled with thoughts of suicide for many years, until one day she came to a place where she was able to completely forgive herself for her perceived wrong, and receive God's unconditional love and grace into her life.

It was only at that point that she was able to receive the mercy and love of God into her life. Releasing forgiveness toward herself, and standing on God's Word about who she was in Christ, was not a one-time event but something she had to do over and over again until the voice of self-hatred and suicide left.

People who have tried to commit suicide are struggling with unresolved issues of self-hatred, condemnation, guilt, shame, and other negative emotions. Because they never resolved their own personal dilemmas in a constructive way, negative emotions became a stronghold in their lives.

NO CONDEMNATION

A person struggling with condemnation usually has very little mercy and forgiveness in operation toward themselves. Sometimes they are hard on themselves and others. They are hard on others because that same voice of condemnation gets projected and transferred onto other people.

Condemnation, however, is not from God. The Bible states in Romans 8:1, "There is therefore now no condemnation to them which are in Christ Jesus, who walk not after the flesh, but after the Spirit."

The second half of this verse is the condition necessary for the promise to be experienced. When you walk after the flesh, (i.e. self-hate, unforgiveness, negative emotions) you fall under condemnation because you are giving negative feelings legal precedence in your life. When you walk after the Spirit, which is love, joy, peace, patience, kindness, gentleness, and a sound mind, you free yourself from the bondage of condemnation.

The fruit of the Spirit operating in a person's life will always triumph over the voice of condemnation, guilt, or self-hate.

One incident of condemnation in the Bible almost led to a stoning but Jesus saved the day. In the book of John, Jesus told the accusers of the woman caught in adultery, " . . . He that is without sin among you, let him first cast a stone at her" (John 8:7). Not a single person in the crowd that day was able to cast a stone at her, because no one was without sin.

Next, you can see the compassion of Jesus in operation when He told this same woman that He did not condemn her either. We read further in John 8:10-11, "' . . . Woman, where are those thine accusers? hath no man condemned thee?' She said, 'No man, Lord. And Jesus said unto her, Neither do I condemn thee: go, and sin no more.'"

My assertion is that if Jesus does not condemn you, then what good does it do to condemn yourself, condemn others, or allow others to condemn you? Jesus came to save the world, not to condemn the world. His message was one of love and mercy, not condemnation, guilt and hatred.

Romans 8:33-34 states, "Who shall lay any thing to the charge of God's elect? It is God that justifieth. Who is he that condemeth? It is Christ that died, yea rather, that is risen again, who is even at the right hand of God, who also maketh intercession for us."

Because you are justified (freed from condemnation) through your faith in God, which originates in the spiritual realm first, man cannot condemn you (technically speaking) in the natural realm unless you receive the condemnation unto yourself, out of your own free will and lack of knowledge.

Instead of living in condemnation, choose the endless rivers of mercy and grace that is found at the cross of Christ. Jesus Christ gives mercy and grace (without cost) to anyone who will simply believe that He is the son of the living God.

SONGS OF DELIVERANCE

Jesus is not condemning you for failure, loss, or personal sin. Quite the contrary, He is interceding for your deliverance in the Heavenly realm. Psalm 32:7 says, "Thou art my hiding place; thou shalt preserve me from trouble; thou shalt compass me about with songs of deliverance."

Jesus is praying that you will stay strong and use your faith in the midst of every crisis. He told Peter in Luke 22:31-32, ". . . Simon, Simon, behold, Satan hath desired to have you, that he may sift you as wheat: But I have prayed for thee, that thy faith fail not: and when thou art converted, strengthen thy brethren."

Jesus knew the struggles that Peter would experience and had prayed in advance that Peter's faith would not fail him. Just as Jesus prayed for Peter in advance of his crisis, Jesus has prayed for you in advance of your tragedy, that your faith would not fail you. Remember that your victory over grief is a finished work of the Cross here on earth. Your part is to enter into that finished work by faith, and in doing so, you will be establishing God's Kingdom, "on earth as is it in Heaven." (See Matthew 6:10.)

The Lord showed me that when you condemn yourself, you have come into agreement with the father of lies, who is Satan. This activates his power. Secondly, you put yourself in the place of God and this quenches His power. Either way, you are giving life and power to the dark kingdom, and at the same time, you are short-circuiting power from God's kingdom.

YOUR REAL ENEMY

Satan is your real enemy. He came to bring death and destruction to God's people. John 10:10 says, "The thief cometh not, but for to steal, and to kill, and to destroy: I am come that they might have life, and that they might have it more abundantly." In John 8:44, Jesus exposed who the real enemy is when He said, "Ye are of your father the devil, and the lusts of your father ye will do. He was a murderer from the beginning, and abode not in the truth, because there is no truth in him. When he speaketh a lie, he speaketh of his own: for he is a liar, and the father of it."

Satan is the father and originator of all lies as far back as the Garden of Eden when he deceived Adam and Eve into eating from the tree of the knowledge of good and evil.

The New Testament goes on to explain in the book of Ephesians that you do not wrestle with flesh and blood, but with principalities and powers and rulers of darkness. Therefore, you should, "Be sober, be vigilant; because your adversary the devil, as a roaring lion, walketh about, seeking whom he may devour. Whom resist steadfast in the faith, knowing that the same afflictions are accomplished in your brethren that are in the world" (1 Peter 5:8-9).

In the book of Revelation, Satan is referred to as the accuser of the brethren (Revelation 12:10). As an accuser, he is eager and willing to accommodate you with condemning and accusing thoughts when you lose a loved one, when you fail, or when you are in a weakened emotional state.

Knowing the Word of God, and speaking faith filled words over your life, will increase your faith and enable you to separate the truth you know from the lies of the enemy that you are tempted to believe.

Remember that when you are weak and wounded, it is easy to believe a lie. Satan will always come when your guard is down.

ENCOURAGING WORDS

Positive, faith-filled words can be used as great encouragement to help another individual. You may be the very person God will send in someone else's life to give them the gift of encouraging words. The Bible says, "A word fitly spoken and in due season is like apples of gold in settings of silver" (Proverbs 25:11 AMP).

God can use your words to impact someone else's life. Words of encouragement that are timely and spoken from the heart can help to lift a person out of the depths of despair and depression, and give them hope. Words spoken from the heart to another individual can be therapeutic, healing and nurturing. One word from God can change a person's life.

When you think about it, God has probably spoken things to you throughout your life, whether through His Word, through a conversation or sermon, through a teacher or mentor, through a book, or through prophecy. Though you may not remember them or constantly dwell on those words, they are still inside of you, stored in your memory.

The Holy Spirit will remind you of these life-changing words when you need them the most. They could be the very words that keep you going, revive your hope, encourage you when you are downtrodden, or even give you a reason to keep on living in the midst of a terrible crisis.

When I think of how powerful encouraging words can be, I think of a situation involving a brave young man named Jason who was involved in a terrible car crash while visiting friends in another country. Because the accident occurred along a less traveled country road, it took the ambulance an entire hour before it arrived at the accident scene.

Jason was bleeding profusely with severe head injuries and was losing consciousness as he and others waited for help to arrive. In the midst of all of the chaos, Jason remembered an encouraging word that had been spoken over his life several years earlier by a minister at his church.

The minister prayed over him and said, "I don't know what this is suppose to mean but I see you on a porch with your family. You are gray-headed and much older, and your grandchildren are playing all around while you and your wife are sitting on the porch. All of you seem very happy, and you are laughing and enjoying each other's company. I see the end of your life and it is very good."

While he was literally hanging on for his life, Jason remembered those encouraging words from the past and he knew that he would not die that day, but would live long and live strong. He held on to those words while he was fighting for his life.

They gave him the strength to fight against the thoughts in his mind that he would die that day. Those same words gave him hope and the will to fight to stay conscious until the paramedics arrived.

Today, Jason and his new bride are living out their dreams and making an impact in the lives of others. God used that word of encouragement at a very strategic moment in his life.

My friend Percine made this comment, *"With encouraging words should come the commitment to see that person through to the place of healing—speaking words of faith in God to comfort and heal them. Sometimes just sitting or crying with the one who is hurting helps them."*

In her book entitled, *Silver Boxes*, Florence Littauer writes, " . . . when we reflect on the turning points in our lives, we often find they came at the encouragement of a person who believed in us, a person who took the time and perhaps the risk to give a portion of himself to someone in need."[3]

PRAYING OVER YOURSELF

Prayer is important in your relationship with God, but prayer is also a powerful weapon that should be used to help you resist spiritual attacks against your mind. Pray over yourself or have someone else pray with you when you are feeling discouraged or when your mind is being bombarded with negative thoughts.

Agreement prayers are some of the most powerful and effective prayers that you can pray because one person praying can put a thousand to flight, and two people praying can put ten thousand to flight when it comes to standing against the dark kingdom. (See Deuteronomy 32:30.) Praying this simple prayer below will help to strengthen and encourage you when you are struggling with your emotions:

Dear Lord, I come before you in the name of Jesus. I humble my heart before you and ask you to forgive me for believing lies about myself. You said in your Word that there is no condemnation for those who are in Christ Jesus. Christ lives in me; therefore, I refuse to listen to the voice of condemnation, guilt, and self-hatred any longer.

I resist the enemy and release myself from all negative emotions. They do not belong to me. I send them back to the pit where they came from.

Lord, I ask you to forgive me for hating myself, or blaming myself or anyone else for what has happened. I understand that no one is perfect except Jesus, and I understand that you do not require perfection from me; you accept me just as I am. You said in your Word that you are looking for a humble and contrite heart from which you would never despise nor turn away.

> *I confess that I do not have a spirit of fear but of love, power, and a calm, sound mind. Dear Lord, establish my thoughts and heal my damaged emotions by the Word of your power.*
>
> *Help me to accept what has happened without blaming or condemning anyone. Purify my mind, my heart, and my soul. Renew a right spirit within me. Help me to be strong and not give up, and help me to keep my eyes stayed upon You that I may have perfect peace always, in Jesus' name. Amen.*

GUILT

Another common grief emotion is guilt. For some time after Stephanie died, I constantly thought of what I could have done differently or how I could have prevented her death. Studies indicate that feelings of inadequacy or questions about how you could have been a better mother or father are normal for parents who lose a child. What I came to realize, though, is how needless it was to feel this way because the guilt that I felt as a parent could not change the past nor bring my daughter back to life. I was wasting mental energy that could have been better spent on overcoming grief.

Guilt produces nagging thoughts that keep you burdened with a sense of responsibility for mistakes you cannot correct.

The tendency to have guilt is especially true for those who experienced a breech in relationship. Those who have lost someone dear often feel it an honor—even a responsibility—to carry the burden of grief and to suffer indefinitely, as if to pay some type of self-imposed debt. You begin to believe that you owe your lost loved one some type of penance because he or she died and you did not. If this is true in your life, I pray that God would lift this false burden from you.

SHAME

Even though you may feel overwhelming shame due to your loss, you must resist the tendency to believe that you are unworthy, unacceptable, or most of all, a worthless human being. Based on what you choose to believe about yourself, you can be your own worst enemy during this time.

The voice of shame makes you say to yourself, "I am flawed, I am a mistake, I am defective, and I am a bad person." Because of negative past experiences in life, some people will believe these lies. The thing to remember is that even though bad things may have happened in your life, it does not make you a bad person. Always remember that you are a wonderful and unique individual who has purpose and meaning in life.

Shame is a feeling of heaviness—like a black cloud that follows you wherever you go. Shame is an emotional weight that you cannot afford to carry around while you are grieving. ***Shame will always be an unspoken and invisible wall that stands between you and your emotional healing.*** In his book, *Facing Shame,* Merle Fossum defines shame as,

"A persuasive sense of shame is the ongoing premise that one is fundamentally bad, inadequate, defective, unworthy or not fully valid as a human being."[4]

Grief may intensify and spike feelings of shame that may have already been lying dormant in a person's life before their loss.

Feelings of guilt and shame are closely related. You feel guilt when you have done something wrong or when you think you have done something wrong. You feel shame when you feel that something about you is inherently wrong. How do you overcome shame? For me, the starting point was to believe and receive the grace of God into my life.

Grace is God's unmerited favor extended in unconditional love and endless mercy toward you. Grace replaces your futile, human attempt to become acceptable and worthwhile in your own strength, for God's grace offers total acceptance, unmerited favor, and unconditional love. According to author Lewis B. Smedes, in his book entitled, *Shame and Grace*, he writes that "Grace is the beginning of our healing because it offers the one thing we need most: to be accepted without regard to whether we are acceptable. Grace stands for gift; it is the gift of being accepted before we become acceptable."[5]

SELF-HATE

As explained earlier in this chapter, self-hate can be a very destructive emotion. Unresolved issues of guilt, blame, condemnation, and shame can all lead to self-hate. The combination and complexity of these mixed emotions can perpetuate and lead to serious emotional problems; therefore, they should be dealt with and brought to resolution as soon as possible.

Most people do not understand the seriousness of self-hate; and if they did, they would probably not admit that they have a problem in this area. For most people, hating yourself is embarrassing to confess, to say the least. This is probably why it remains a secret in the lives of many. Even though feelings of self-hate may remain anonymous, self-hate is a sin against God. When you hate yourself, you hate God because He created you in His likeness and image.

When you hate yourself, you dishonor the unique and wonderful individual that God created. Ephesians 2:10 says, "For we are His workmanship, created in Christ Jesus unto good works, which God hath before ordained that we should walk in them." *Remember that you are a beautiful and wonderful work of art (a masterpiece), created by God in Christ Jesus. Being healed from grief requires that you see yourself the way God sees you.* Seeing yourself the way God sees you will require that you forgive yourself of any blame or guilt (whether it is real or imagined) that you may feel, and learn how to truly love—the unique "you" that God created.

The Great Commandment (See Mark 12:29-31.) is not just that you love God, but that you also love yourself as well. Once you allow God to heal your damaged emotions, then the love of God that has been shed abroad in your heart by the Holy Ghost (See Romans 5:5.) can be freely released to love God, love others, and love yourself. Love is a life changing force that can mend and heal your broken heart and wash away any negativity in your life.

Being loved, loving yourself, and receiving God's love is vitally important to your healing and sense of well being as a person.

MY BATTLE WITH FEAR

It happened like clockwork almost every night. After Stephanie died, I began to battle tormenting thoughts of fear. I felt an evil presence in my home. I sensed the spirit of death all around me. No matter how deep of a sleep I was in, I would automatically wake up around three o'clock in the morning and I would stay wide-awake for hours and hours. As I lay in bed thinking about the details of Stephanie's death, I would become more and more afraid—constantly thinking of the night she died, and running different scenarios through my mind of what could have possibly happened in the moments before her death.

A fearful mind is a troubled mind, but a mind fixed upon the Word of God is one that is at peace. Isaiah 26:3 states, "Thou wilt keep him in perfect peace, whose mind is stayed on thee: because he trusteth in thee." The peace that God gives is a supernatural peace that is not based on outside forces, the condition of your life, or the circumstances you are facing at the moment.

I was too embarrassed to tell anyone about my battle with fear, and I did not want to validate my fears by talking about what I was experiencing. Instead, I kept silent. I prayed, I quoted scriptures, I kept the lights on, I played worship music, friends loaned me their pet dog for company; someone stayed with me around the clock. No matter what I tried, my struggle with fear did not go away until I decided to do something proactive.

FEAR EXPOSED

People struggle with all sorts of fears but few speak about fear as it relates to grief. Those who have lost loved ones are said to be prone to the fear of dying themselves. Studies indicate that if a child's parent died a premature death, that child may have an overwhelming fear all his life that he too will die at a premature age. Many of these fears become self-fulfilling prophecies.

In 2 Timothy 1:7 (AMP), the Bible says, "for God did not give us a spirit of timidity (of cowardice, of craven and cringing and fawning fear), but [He has given us a spirit] of power and of love and of calm and well-balanced mind and discipline and self-control."

You received a calm and well-balanced mind at salvation. You did not receive a spirit of timidity, cowardice, or cringing fear. Therefore, any thoughts, feelings, emotions or experiences that produce fear, anxiety, or panic are not from God and should be challenged with the Word of God.

FEAR DEFINED

Webster's Dictionary defines *fear* as "*a feeling or expectation of the worst.*"[6] Even though you cannot see fear with your naked eye, you can discern the effect that fear has on an individual by observing his or her actions and words.

Fear, however, is more than a feeling or a painful grief emotion. The Bible refers to fear as a spirit. Not being able to see fear with your naked eye does not negate its reality and ability to torment you. Fear is like a mirage, which is an image that is not real but seems real. Fear is sometimes referred to as false evidence appearing real. The evidence that fear will present to your mind is only circumstantial—it is not the whole truth—it may be an established fact—even half a fact—but it is still not the whole truth.

Fear is elusive and sometimes difficult to detect in an individual, but most people can discern for themselves whether or not fear is at the root of how they think, feel, or respond. If you do not know for sure if fear is at the root of your thinking and responses in life, ask the Lord and He will show you.

TAKE AUTHORITY

One of the ways that you overcome fear is by exercising your God-given authority over the voice of fear. Jesus Christ delegated His authority to all believers when He came to the earth over 2000 years ago to establish His Kingdom in the heart of man. Jesus said in Luke 10:19, "Behold, I give unto you power to tread on serpents and scorpions, and over all the power of the enemy: and nothing shall by any means hurt you." The authority Jesus spoke of was spiritual authority that is activated when you release your faith in what He said. You have the power within you to overcome fear because the Greater One lives in you! (See 1 John 4:4.)

However, when you take a stand against fear, just thinking of a scripture, or replacing fearful emotions with some other random thought, will not work. You have merely made mental assent when you are thinking of the Word of God but not speaking the Word of God.

The power of God is in the spoken Word, not in man's natural words or natural thoughts. Hebrews 4:12 states, "The Word of God is quick, and powerful, and sharper than any two-edged sword, piercing even to the dividing asunder of soul and spirit, and of the joints and marrow, and is a discerner of the thoughts and intents of the heart."

The Word of God is alive, with energy, properties, abilities, and substance that have a supernatural strength within them. When you speak forth the word of God, releasing your faith in what you have said, it creates a force and energy powerful enough to change the atmosphere.

One of the ways that you overcome the spirit of fear is by consistently speaking faith-filled words, opposed to allowing fearful thoughts and feelings to torment your mind. For instance, when I became fearful in the middle of the night, I made myself sit up in bed and pray the Word of God (out loud) until peace came. Rolling over in the bed and pulling the covers over my head would not have given me victory over fear.

God has promised you, His child, that no matter what type of fear you are facing, He will deliver you from it *all*. (See Psalm 34:4.) Bringing your fears out into the open by telling a trusted person who knows the Word of God will be helpful. Find someone who is not prone to fear themselves, but someone who can pray with you in faith and give you good advice. Sometimes, just talking with someone else about your fears can remove much of the mysterious power that fear has in your mind.

KEEP RESISTING

Instead of succumbing to fear, I had to resist the spirit of fear. The Bible says to submit yourself to God, resist the devil and he will flee from you (James 4:7). Webster's Dictionary defines *resist* as to "*fight against, to oppose, to combat, to repel, or to withstand the force or effect of.*"[7] Allowing fear to reside in your life gives Satan a doorway—a foothold—legal ground to continue to torment your mind.

Resisting fear is an active, rather than passive, position you take against the forces of Satan. Again, it is a spiritual position you uphold through faith in God and what He said in His Word. You resist fear by refusing to meditate on fearful thoughts or by allowing yourself to overreact to fearful emotions or situations. In other words, do not act on what you are feeling if what you are feeling does not line up with the Word of God or His principles.

CONTROL YOUR THOUGHTS

One tactic of the enemy is to try and establish a foothold in your life, beginning with your thoughts. When you entertain thoughts of fear, you are opening your mind to the dark kingdom. The battle will always begin in your mind because thoughts are seeds. If you meditate on the seed (or thoughts) of fear, they will begin to germinate and grow. But if you meditate on the Word of God and think upon things that are positive and peaceful, faith and peace will grow and increase.

Standing against fear meant that I had to take control of my thoughts instead of letting them go the way of least resistance. The Bible says to bring every thought captive into the obedience of Christ. (See 1 Corinthians 10:5.) Take control of your thoughts the moment you begin thinking about anything that is fearful or negative.

You can choose what you think about, and whether or not you will allow your mind to meditate on thoughts of fear or thoughts of faith. The Apostle Paul said in Philippians 4:8, "Finally, brethren, whatsover things are true, whatsoever things are honest, whatsoever things are just, whatsoever things are pure, whatsoever things are lovely, whatsoever things are of good report; if there be any virtue, and if there be any praise, think on these things."

Instead of meditating on fearful, negative, or painful thoughts, think positive thoughts—think higher thoughts—and meditate daily on the Word of God. This approach takes practice and discipline but the results can be life changing.

THE WORD – YOUR ROADMAP FOR LIVING

A wounded person is very susceptible to wrong thinking but knowing the Word of God will help you to maintain right thinking. Knowing the Word of God helped to stabilize my thought life in spite of how unsteady my emotions were after Stephanie's death. The Word works like a plumb line, correctly applying truth against the backdrop of your life to alert you of anything that would cause you to veer off course in your mind or actions. The Word of God reveals and sheds light on anything that lies in secret—the hidden recesses of your soul—distorted thought processes and hurtful experiences that are suppressed within your memory files.

The Word of God can pierce and divide between soul and spirit, properly discerning between truth and lies, light and darkness. Knowing the Word can help you to plainly differentiate what is false and what is true about your situation, about yourself, about other people, and about God.

Becoming familiar with the Word of God should not be done in an effort to become self-righteous, but in order for you to rightly divide the "roadmap for living" that God left for you to read and believe. ***Knowing and applying the Word of God in every situation you face will be a vital key to your recovery from grief.***

When tribulation comes into your life, the Word of God (if illuminated in your mind and settled in your heart) will empower you to stand firm against any attack of the enemy. As an anchor keeps a ship from drifting away, so too, the Word of God will keep your mind from drifting toward painful and fearful emotions, thoughts, or feelings. As you continue in the Word, your mind will begin to choose thoughts of peace and thoughts that are pure, holy, and lovely.

THE HOLY SPIRIT

Another advantage to knowing the Word of God is that in any type of crisis, the Holy Spirit will quickly bring God's Word to your remembrance. If God's Word is not abiding within you, the Holy Spirit has nothing from which to draw upon. However, if the Word of God abides within you, the Holy Spirit's purpose is to help recall and remind you of *all* of the Words of Jesus.

But the Comforter (Counselor, Helper, Intercessor, Advocate, Strengthener, Standby), the Holy Spirit, Whom the Father will send in My name [in My place, to represent Me and act on My behalf], He will teach you all things. And He will cause you to recall (will remind you of, bring to your remembrance) everything I have told you. John 14:26 (AMP)

It bears repeating that the Word of God hidden in your heart will act as a guard to help detect any counterfeit thoughts, feelings, and emotions. This is important when you are grieving because the battlefield of grief is located in your mind, where all of these elements exist. The real battle over grief and loss is fought inside your mind; therefore, what you accept as truth will not only determine your grief journey, but your entire course in life.

COMPELLING THOUGHTS
Even when you know the Word, painful emotions and thoughts will still be something you have to sort through and deal with on a daily basis. If your grief has been caused by the death of a loved one, you may have thought or said one or more of the following statements:

It was my fault—I should have done more!
Something must be wrong with me. Everyone I love dies!

I hate myself. I am nothing but a loser and a failure!

I bet my parents wish I had died instead of my sister!

I can't stand to live this way . . . it would be easier if I were dead!

Negative thoughts can seem overwhelming and compelling—even seductive at times. The voice of death is very seductive. When life brings one to this point, an extremely wounded person may need professional help before recovery can be realized. Intervention of some type may be necessary. Knowing when to get help is just as important as getting the help itself. Do not wait until it is too late. If you are contemplating suicide, no one expects you to overcome these emotional problems alone. Please ask for help.

How do you free yourself from thoughts of suicide? How do you free yourself from overwhelming thoughts that plague your mind and trigger negative emotions when least expected? How do you prevent negative grief emotions from ruling your life?

Make a quality decision that you are going to make it through to the other side of pain and grief. Embrace the process of grief and work through these painful emotions, using the Word of God as your guide. This is a decision every person who has suffered loss must make. The process may seem overwhelming at first, but the payoff (healing and freedom) in the end is worth the time and effort you had to invest in yourself. Otherwise, negative emotions that are left unattended and unresolved will never heal. They will only mushroom in your mind. For a time, you may be able to push them out of your mind but you cannot push them out of your life.

Understanding the process of grief emotions, being able to recognize them as they arise, and learning how to constructively sort through them will take you to a place of healing without the threat of getting stuck in grief. How you cope with your loss as you deal with your thoughts and feelings is critical to your recovery. ***Painful emotions do not go away simply because you refuse to face them.***

PERFECT LOVE

Love is your answer. One of the ways that you overcome fear and negative emotions is through the power of love. Not just any love, but perfect love—God's love. 1 John 4:18 states that, "There is no fear in love; but perfect love casteth out fear; because fear hath torment. He that feareth is not made perfect in love."

God the Father is the essence and total fulfillment of love. His love is supernatural and it lasts forever. His love for you is not based on your performance or good works but is based on what He has done through His son Jesus Christ. He so loved the world that He gave His only begotten Son to save you, not to condemn you.

God uses others to love you—your families, your children, your mate, and your friends—but ultimately, your primary source of love should first come from Him. Because God is love, He is the perfect expression and exact representation of love.

The Creator's love is all-powerful, never-ending, and has no possibility of failure or disappointment. When you begin to focus on the love of God and not on your fears, peace and joy will be restored to your life. Focusing on the love of God may seem like a small thing but it can transform your life. When you are hurting, unconditional love is what you need more than anything else.

Your heart can be filled with the love of God during fellowship and intimate times with the Lord. When you are in His presence, He pours His unfailing love into your wounded and fearful heart. Overcoming the pain of loss requires that you spend quality time with your Father in order to bask (which means to lie around, laze around, stretch out, relax) in His love.

Fear brings with it punishment and torment. But God's love brings peace, reassurance, and comfort. Love is the key that unlocks everything!

FIVE STAGES OF GRIEF

Many feelings surface during the normal grief process and are all part of your natural healing response. Having an understanding of each of these will help you better deal with them, as you will most likely face each one of them (and more) at some time or another during your journey to healing. There were five major areas of grief that I read about and had firsthand experience with during my own grief journey. I have listed them separately for you to consider:

1) Shock and Denial: No one wants to experience shock, but for someone who has been traumatized when tragic loss occurs, it is nature's way of protecting you from being destroyed emotionally by devastating news.

When you are in shock, you may not be able to cry, accept, or even acknowledge your loss. I remember how puzzled others were that I barely cried at my daughter's funeral. Your inability to cry, to accept, or acknowledge your loss may be thought of as strange and almost offensive to some.

How good of God to have created this safety net, or mental time out, until your mind and emotions have a chance to adjust and catch up with the reality of your loss. Once you come out of shock, and you realize the extent of your loss, anger is next on the list. Anger is a normal feeling to have when you are grieving, so do not feel guilty about being angry.

2) Anger: Anger in grief is an indication that you are past shock and denial and are moving forward in the grieving process. Anger is a natural reaction to the unfairness of loss and to the sense of injustice that loss brings. Anger develops because of the unfairness you feel that you have personally suffered a horrific loss instead of someone else. You may experience feelings of wanting to fight back or getting even with someone.

I experienced feelings of anger toward my daughter because I felt that she did not fight hard enough to stay alive, and because she did not wake me during the night of her struggle. I was angry because I did not have the opportunity to help her or say good-bye to her before she died.

Eventually, I had to work through these feelings and release them to God in prayer. Do not be afraid or embarrassed about your anger, but learn to express your anger in a positive way, such as journaling how you feel. As mentioned in the previous chapter, expressing your thoughts and feelings on paper is a healthy way to release pent up anger and unresolved grief emotions.

If journaling seems too introspective, verbalizing your anger may help. Scream into a pillow if necessary, or hit a punching bag. Let your anger out in safe ways that do not involve hurting or attacking other people. Unresolved anger only intensifies over time and will eventually lead to some type of unplanned outburst. The key is to give yourself permission to feel anger, while at the same time learning how to control your anger responses.

Since anger is a normal part of the grieving process, grief survivors should not be looked down upon or ostracized because they are dealing with anger issues. Instead, they should be prayed for and lovingly supported by family and friends. Unconditional love and acceptance from others can disarm an angry person, and can become a significant source of comfort and healing to a hurting person.

3) Bargaining: You can sway from intense feelings of anger to trying to make deals with God, to avoiding your loss altogether. This is called bargaining, which is another stage of grief that some people experience. This stage usually takes place before loss occurs, but can also occur after loss. If your loved one is ill, you may try to make deals with him or her or with God. Forms of bargaining include: making promises, wishing for things to be different, or praying for your loved one to return.

You may try to negotiate with God or others to change your situation. An example of bargaining is during the breakup of a marriage, you make unrealistic promises in order to keep a mate in the relationship. Bargaining is a wasted attempt to stay in control of your circumstances, and to avoid accepting the reality of your loss. Once you have exhausted all of your attempts to control the inevitable, and it has not worked, your next response is usually one of deep despair and depression.

4) Depression: This stage consists of overwhelming feelings of hopelessness, frustration, bitterness, and self-pity. If you have lost a loved one, it also includes mourning the loss of the person as well as the hopes, dreams, and plans you had for that individual. During this stage, you may feel a lack of control; you may also feel numb and perhaps even suicidal.

Depression is such a heavy emotional weight that if allowed to rule your life, you will never experience true healing. You will become part of the masses of people who are currently stuck in a grief mode, living in the shadows of their loss. Most people do not understand the connection between properly grieving their losses in order to reach a place of emotional well-being. Grieving is a very important process, not just to go through but also to complete.

The best way out of depression is to accept (with total abandonment) what happened, which is one of the final stages of recovery. Coming to terms with your loss removes depression and produces a mind at rest and at peace with life.

5) Acceptance: This stage is where you have accepted the reality of your loss. You have come to the place where you have fully accepted what has happened. Acceptance is where you make peace with your loss, you make peace with your past, and you genuinely accept what has occurred. You no longer carry your loss as a heavy burden. You are able to put closure on what has happened. You are able to think about your loss without emotional crying, without emotional pain, or without a sick feeling in the pit of your stomach.

Acceptance is not only finding the good that can come out of the pain of loss, but through it, you also find comfort and healing. In acceptance, your goals turn toward personal and spiritual growth and finding out what God has for you in the future. Acceptance is about moving on with your life.

IDENTIFY YOUR FEELINGS

Resolving damaged grief emotions requires that you are first willing to identify and get in touch with your feelings. If you feel overwhelmed, or if you feel that your emotions are too complicated to resolve alone, you may need professional counseling or grief therapy. Pretending that any of these issues discussed do not affect you will only prolong your healing and complicate your recovery. Seeking help is an acceptable and positive step in the right direction. Everyone needs help once in a while.

Simply talking to someone you trust concerning your feelings will help immensely, but one of the most liberating things you should do to keep your heart free of negative emotions is to continually walk in a place of forgiveness. Forgiveness is a foundational principle from the Word of God and is absolutely imperative in resolving negative grief emotions.

Keep your heart free of anger, offenses, bitterness, and unforgiveness, as you are moving forward in your grief journey. (See more about this topic in forgiveness chapter.)

SUMMING IT UP

Even though you may feel that you have experienced every negative emotion known to man, you must constructively process these feelings and allow God to heal the pain of your loss. In John 5:12, Jesus told the sick man at the Pool of Bethesda who had waited thirty-eight years for his healing,

"Take up thy bed, and walk." There comes a time that you must go forth despite how you feel. As you go forth, you will heal.

This whole process is a step-by-step, day-by-day walk that requires a determination to see it through to completion. Being able to move forward and to set new goals for your future is a sure sign that you are healing. Remember that God will customize a new life for you if you let Him.

Processing grief means that you have been able to assimilate your loss as you pass through the different stages of grief, and at the same time, resolve the myriad of grief emotions that you feel. It also means that you are intentional about working toward your own recovery. It means that you are deliberate about pursuing your life goals, along with being genuinely ready to reinvest in your future.

The Apostle Paul said in Philippians 3:13-14, " . . . but this one thing I do, forgetting those things which are behind, and reaching forth unto those things which are before, I press toward the mark for the prize of the high calling of God in Christ Jesus." Pressing toward new goals in life will require effort on your part, but there is a prize for putting continuous effort into your grief journey. There is a payoff for pressing forth because your journey does have a destination!

Grief Emotions Prayer:

Dear Heavenly Father,

I give all of my feelings and emotions to you Lord. Please forgive me for thinking negative thoughts and believing lies from the enemy. I renounce every thought in my life that is not of you. I confess that I have the mind of Christ and that the washing of Your Word renews my thinking. I confess that I am anxious for nothing and that in all things, through prayer and supplication, I will make my requests known unto you, and the peace of God that surpasses all understanding will rule and reign in my heart and mind in Christ Jesus. Thank you for filling my mind with peace.

Lord, you said in Romans 12:2 not to be conformed to this world but be transformed by the renewing of my mind that I may know the good, pleasing, and perfect will of God. I confess that my mind is renewed, my thinking is clear, and that I am moving into your perfect will for my life. I receive it now, in Jesus' name.

Thank you for healing my emotions and healing my heart. I confess that I am strong in the Lord and the power of your might. I confess that I can do all things through Christ who strengthens me.

I claim victory over my life today, in Jesus' name, Amen.

JOURNAL NOTES

Chapter Five

HEALING DEEP WOUNDS

The Spirit of the Lord is upon Me, because he hath anointed me to preach the gospel to the poor; he hath sent me to heal the brokenhearted, to preach deliverance to the captives, and recovering of sight to the blind, to set at liberty them that are bruised.

Luke 4:18

A picture is said to be worth a thousand words. Several years ago, the Lord gave me a mental picture of what emotional healing from grief requires. When He gave me this picture, I was worshipping Him and seeking Him about my own hurts. I thought the vision that I saw was meant only for me, however, I later found out otherwise.

I was scheduled to speak at a women's conference, but the host church postponed the conference because one of their key leaders had passed away. The memorial service was planned for the day I was to speak. God's timing was perfect though and I knew immediately that what the Lord had given me in prayer was not just for me. This message of healing was not only to be preached, but I was to dramatize it as well. It would serve as a visualization of God's healing for those who were hurting so deeply from this loss. The dramatization went something like this:

The scene opens with a depiction of the Holy of Holies in the middle of the stage, a large wooden cross to the left of the stage, and a grieving area to the right. As the dramatization begins, I am seated to the right of the stage in a mourning chair, crying profusely and clutching a few of my daughter's personal items.

Dressed in all black, I seem inconsolable as I continue to sob and clutch her things. All you hear is my crying. There is no music, no talking. Everything is silent. But before long, an angel comes out from behind the Holy of Holies and walks toward me. He lightly touches my shoulder in a gesture to comfort me. As I sense the angel's presence, I turn slowly to the right as if expecting to see someone. (The Bible says that there are ministering spirits sent to minister to the heirs of salvation. Hebrews 1:14) I see no one but I sense the angel's presence.

Soon the angel beckons me to go with him as he walks toward the Holy of Holies. I want to go with him, but I am not sure what will happen if I leave my mourning place. I appear to be torn—wanting to go with the angel into the presence of God, yet holding on desperately to the memories of my daughter. Finally, I choose to go with the angel.

He leads me into the Holy of Holies and into the presence of God. Then he closes the veil behind me. The only thing the audience can see is a thick cloud of fog coming from the Holy of Holies. When I hear all of Heaven worshipping around the Throne of Grace, I forget all about my sorrow and pain. Completely surrounded by the glory cloud and in the presence of God, I begin to worship the Lord in a way that I had not been able to since my daughter's death. A song of healing is playing while I am behind the veil and while the angel of God dances around the Holy of Holies.

After a few minutes, I come out from behind the veil. Everything about me has changed. Gloriously, my countenance has changed and my clothes (that were once black to signify my state of mourning) are now white to signify freedom and healing. Peace and joy have been restored to my life. I immediately look toward the place where I had been crying—it looks like a shrine to me now. That mourning place represented my grief, my loss, my pain, and my sorrow. Not wanting to go back to that place of pain anymore, I slowly look in the opposite direction and see the cross. Now I know what to do.

The angel is still following me and guiding me. He gently guides me back to the area of mourning, but this time I do not sit and cry as before. Instead, I pick up the personal items that represented my daughter and begin walking toward the cross. The angel continues to guide me as I take her things and lay them at the foot of the cross. The instant that I laid her things at the foot of the cross, something lifted—something changed. The spirit of grief that had tried to crush my soul had been broken. Kneeling at the cross, I make my peace with her death.

The angel stands at attention with his sword, as if to guard me while I am making this exchange. Taking my grief and pain to the cross was something that I had needed to do for a long time but had not been able to do until I was fully taken into God's presence. You cannot get into God's presence without the help of the Holy Spirit. The Bible says in Zechariah 4:6, ". . . Not by might, nor by power, but by my spirit, saith the LORD of hosts." Only the Holy Spirit can lead you into the presence of God, and when He does, it is life changing.

As I am kneeling silently at the foot of the cross with my daughter's possessions in hand, the angel dances in great joy and jubilation while a song of healing and restoration is playing. Then I stand up, still looking to the cross. I have made peace with her death and have released her to God.

The Lord showed me that healing from grief will come as you lay your loved one down at the foot of the cross and release him or her totally, once and for all, into His hands. You cannot do this without continually being in the presence of God, which is why worship is such an important key to your healing. The Bible says that you are to worship Him in Spirit and in truth. (See John 4:23.) You are to worship Him from your heart and your innermost being. Worship comes from deep within a person and is expressed from a heart that knows and loves God. This is what true worship is all about.

While you are in His presence, God will change things inside of you that would not happen in any other way. ***You will find that worship is another part of your spiritual prescription for healing.*** It was while I was in His presence that I knew it was time to do exactly what I did. Now I was ready. It was time.

If you are a grieving parent, you must realize that your child was a gift to you when he or she was born and now you must symbolically give him or her back to God as a gift. Whatever you have lost must be given back to God as a gift.

The cross is your point of contact and serves as a reminder and a safe place that you can release your loved one, or any type of loss, to God. This cannot be done without the Lord's help, and in His timing, but healing will come when you do just that.

Jesus said in Matthew 10:38-39, "And he that taketh not his cross, and followeth after me, is not worthy of me. He that findeth his life shall lose it: and he that loseth his life for my sake shall find it." Losing your life means letting go, dying to the past, and releasing to God that which is now considered loss.

The cross of Calvary represents not only a place of death, but also a place of resurrection. At the cross you will exchange (by faith) your past for the new life that God has for you. You cannot keep them both—one must go in order for you to receive the other. Jesus said in John 11:25-26, ". . . I am the resurrection, and the life: he that believeth in me, though he were dead, yet shall he live: And whosoever liveth and believeth in me shall never die. Believest thou this?"

It will be in dying to your loss with total abandonment that you will live again. The cross of Calvary represents your place of salvation, forgiveness, healing, resurrection, and power.

1 Corinthians 1:18 (AMP) says, "For the story and message of the cross is sheer absurdity and folly to those who are perishing and on their way to perdition, but to us who are being saved it is the [manifestation] of the power of God."

At the cross, there is power for you to be healed, and there is power for you to move on with your life. In dying to your will, you identify with Jesus' death. In rising again to new life, you identify with His resurrection. Your healing from grief begins at the cross, where you can find identification with Christ, and resurrection power in Him alone.

Your healing begins at the Cross!

PHYSICAL WOUNDS

How important is it to be healed from grief? The Lord showed me two perspectives that helped me to understand the importance and urgency for healing. The first perspective had to do with comparing the natural and spiritual realms.

In the natural, if you were seriously injured in a car accident and were not hospitalized in time, you may have died without proper medical attention. If the physical injury were life threatening, emergency surgery would have to be performed to keep you alive. Your physical well-being would require doctors, medicine, specialists, nurses, recovery, and rehabilitation, and maybe even future surgeries. Every second would count if you were to survive!

RECOVERY TIME

After surgery, time in recovery is very important. The more serious the surgery, the more time would be needed in the recovery room. In fact, every patient who undergoes surgery will spend some amount of time in recovery. Recovery is part of your pathway to healing. However, simply being in recovery does not mean that you have fully recovered anymore than saying you are in grief recovery means that you are healed yet.

How much more desperately do you need critical care and attention when you are emotionally wounded and grieving from a tragic loss? How much more should you give yourself permission to embrace the process of grief recovery with the goal of healing in mind?

Because some wounds are physical and visible, they are easier to see and address. Just the same, there are some wounds that are emotional, spiritual, and invisible which cannot be seen with the naked eye and, sometimes because of that, they are often overlooked or ignored.

The key here is to recognize your need for help and cooperate with the pathway of spiritual and emotional healing that God prescribes for you. His pathway is different for each individual. My pathway to healing involved spending time with God, entering His rest and letting my wounds heal, seeking His direction for my life, obeying His leadings (even the slightest), believing Him for total healing, and cooperating with Him in the new environment where He had placed me. It meant totally accepting and surrendering to Him as opposed to resisting His will or pathway for my life.

EMOTIONAL WOUNDS

You are not humanly equipped to handle extreme emotional pain any more than you can tolerate extreme physical pain. This leads me to the second perspective that the Lord showed me in understanding the importance and urgency for healing. Emotional pain and hurt is an indication of an internal wound—something injured on the inside. You cannot see the wound, but it is there just the same.

These internal wounds will eventually produce outward symptoms of negative, self-defeating behaviors. When you put a bandage on outward symptoms of emotional hurt without getting to the root of the problem, the unhealed wound still lies beneath the surface. You may be able to suppress your symptoms for a while, but in time, symptoms will only resurface and cause more problems if the root or inner wound is not revealed, resolved and healed.

RED FLAGS

The Lord showed me that hurt and pain exist because a wound exists. They are indicators, signs, and red flags of a deeper wound. Once the wound is healed, pain and hurt are removed and your emotions can be healed.

Getting to the root of grief (the wound) requires that you have the courage to look below the surface of your pain (the symptoms), no matter how difficult it may seem or how much time and effort it requires. Cry out to God for Him to show you the taproot of your deepest pain and hurt.

FINDING THE ROOT

Healing deep wounds is a vital area to address in grief recovery. Perhaps the reason you are not further along in your healing is because the wound is deeper and more involved than you think. Merely reading self-help books and giving it more time are not the only methods or total answer to grief recovery.

Finding the root cause of the pain is a significant part of the answer and a foundational step toward recovery. God cannot do what He wants in your life if you remain in denial about suppressed inner pain, or if you are afraid to revisit past hurts.

A major key to recovery is to first become honest with yourself and others about how you are doing, and about what is going on in your life and in your heart. Become transparent with others and stay open to the pathway that God will use to heal you. Was it not Shakespeare who said, "To thine own self be true."[1] As you are working through grief, think of it as a personal investment in yourself. You are worth it.

REMOVING THE MASK

After Stephanie's death, I tried to pick up the pieces as best I could, but eventually the grief that I was going through began to collide with old wounds from my past. I reached a point where I could not suppress them anymore, and I could not pretend that everything was okay. These unhealed areas in my life were affecting everything about me—my personal life, my finances, my relationships, my ministry; even my relationship with God was affected. But the Lord in His great wisdom allowed me to come to the end of myself because it was not until I came to the end of myself that I was able to see the reality of what was really happening in my life. My eyes were opened to just how deeply I had been wounded.

If you are not actively seeking help and allowing God to work in your life, unresolved grief, combined with past hurts will only become more complicated. When your internal pain tank fills up, so to speak, emotional hurts begin to spill over into other areas of your life. At some point, these issues must be resolved or they will only cause you more distress and long-term problems. When you decide to remove the mask and all pretense of having it all together, your life will begin to change for the better.

OUT OF CONTROL

As I began to see my life spiraling out of control, the Lord made a provision for me to move to another city. I found a job that God soon began to use as a tool, or classroom if you will, to help me see the hidden issues and hurts in my life that He wanted to heal (which required my cooperation). The Lord selected this time while I was in a different environment for me to fully grieve the loss of my daughter. I am not advocating that you pick up and move to another city to help with your grief. Only do what God leads you to do in your process of healing.

INTERIOR STORM

When you are grieving, you need time to sort through the "interior storm" that is taking a toll on your emotions. You need time to sort through the questions of your emotional highs and lows in order to resolve all of your pain issues.

Finding out about grief, and allowing for time to grieve, is mandatory if you are going to have a healthy, positive response to loss. Some people are too busy to allow grief the necessary time to filter through their systems.

Because you heal from the inside out, Jesus said to clean the inside of the cup and the outside would take care of itself. (See Matthew 23:26.) Healthy grieving has the same effect as cleaning "inside the cup" as Jesus recommended. ***But keep in mind that grieving is only productive when healing is your ultimate goal.***

Otherwise, you risk becoming trapped in a grief tunnel with no end in sight. You should take as much time as needed to grieve, but the process of grief should always take you to the next level of acceptance and healing. Remember that there is a time to grieve and there is a time to heal.

Ecclesiastes 3:1 states, "To every thing there is a season, and a time to every purpose under the heaven:" Verse three goes on to say that there is a time to heal. You may feel that you will never heal from your loss, or that you will never be the same again, but there is a pre-ordained, pre-set time given by God for your healing.

When God moved me to another city, I recognized that this would be the time and the place that I would not only grieve the loss of my daughter, but I would heal and become whole again.

Stand on God's Word and trust in God's timing. Your Heavenly Father knows the exact moment when you are prepared and ready to fully process the pain of grief out of your heart and out of your life. He will seize that moment for you!

COOPERATE WITH GOD

What is your part in all of this? Your part is to cooperate with God. Start by taking whatever time is necessary to empty your "pain tank." Hiding or suppressing your emotional pain while God is allowing everything possible in your life to bring these issues to the surface is an exercise in futility. Allow God to reveal what He wants in your life without resisting Him, because what He reveals, He heals.

While you should not suppress your emotions, do not allow your emotions to totally spiral out of control. Remember that the fruit of the Spirit is love, joy, peace, patience, kindness, goodness and self-control.

The Lord revealed to me that if I had yielded fully to my emotions during my season of grieving, I would have lost all the spiritual ground that I had gained through the years of serving Him, studying His Word, and walking in His will. The healing process would have been delayed, if not stopped altogether. I would have been stuck in grief had I allowed my emotions to run rampant.

WHAT GOD ALLOWS

The Lord will allow situations, problems, needs, circumstances, and interactions with other people as spiritual tools to help refine your character and purge away the pain of grief and issues from your past. As mentioned earlier, God may permit something as ordinary as challenges at your workplace to help bring you to a greater level of spiritual growth, maturity, and healing. If you are experiencing anything of this nature, it may help you to realize that the Lord is more concerned with your character than your comfort.

Many times, the situations you may find yourself in (and their resulting pressures) will cause internal issues to surface. If you will be alert to your actions and reactions that have come to light, then the Lord will teach you what you need to do in the healing process.

This can include something as basic as recognizing ungodly behavior on your part, confessing it, and repenting of (falling out of agreement with) that particular behavior. It may help to talk to a trusted, mature Christian friend or to even seek professional counseling and/or prayer ministry. I have listed some of these later in the ministry resource section of this book.

MY STRUGGLE

One example of God bringing the inner issues of my heart to the surface happened at work. I noticed that not long after I began working in a new place of employment, I would sometimes respond to people and situations by either crying too easily, or by overreacting in anger instead of maintaining my composure and humbling myself in every situation.

I remember one time in particular that I left work for the entire day because I had allowed myself to become overly emotional and angry.

As time went on, I began to notice that sometimes my perspective and reactions toward people and situations were being clouded and filtered through deep wounds, unresolved grief, and even past hurts and rejections. The more I tried to suppress this side of me, the more it surfaced. Facing the truth about myself was very difficult—all I wanted to do was run and hide (and sometimes I did). But God wanted me to recognize my ungodly behaviors and begin to respond differently.

I thank God for two understanding bosses, and for a spiritually astute friend, who prayed for me and helped me to understand what was happening, and how humility, repentance, and forgiveness would become my keys to victory. My friend also helped me to understand that running away from this season in my life was not the answer, because God would probably allow this same test to occur someplace else.

There was a war going on inside of me much like the one the Apostle Paul speaks of in Romans 7:18-19, 23-25 which says,

> For I know that in me (that is, in my flesh,) dwelleth no good thing: for to will is present with me; but how to perform that which is good I find not. For

the good that I would I do not: but the evil which I would not, that I do. But I see another law in my members, warring against the law of my mind, and bringing me into captivity to the law of sin which is in my members. O wretched man that I am! who shall deliver me from the body of this death? I thank God through Jesus Christ our Lord. So then with the mind I myself serve the law of God; but with the flesh the law of sin.

Can you relate to Paul's struggle? Even though he accurately described the inner battle that we all face at times, it was through the Apostle Paul's relationship with Jesus that He was able to overcome the weaknesses of his flesh. Because of personal struggles that he could not seem to shake, the Apostle Paul sought the Lord about his inner battles. In doing so, he gained a fresh, understanding into the grace of God. Grace is God's power, influence and favor reflected in your life.

Paul discovered that when you are weak, God's grace has the opportunity to become perfected in your life. So, instead of feeling guilty, afraid or embarrassed about your weaknesses, the key is to embrace your weaknesses and allow the grace of God to give you the strength you need to overcome. When you do this you are overcoming by God's power and not in your own human strength.

With an understanding of how grace works, you can easily see how God allows adversity to perfect you, not to destroy you. Therefore, you must tap into the indwelling power of the Holy Spirit and the grace of God to enable you to overcome the battle from within.

REFINER'S FIRE

The Bible says in Malachi 3:3, "And he shall sit as a refiner and a purifier of silver: and he shall purify the sons of Levi, and purge them as gold and silver, that they may offer unto the LORD an offering in righteousness." Just as a silversmith refines metal by placing it in a hot fire to remove all impurities and dross, so does God allow the fiery furnace of our lives to purify and heal old wounds.

Proverbs 20:30 (NKJV) states, "Blows that hurt cleanse away evil, as do stripes the inner depths of the heart." God will use your response to the pressures and difficulties of life to produce within you a beautiful aroma and sweet smelling fragrance like that of Christ.

When refining silver, the silversmith must hold the silver in the middle of the fire where the flames are the hottest until all the impurities are burned away. The silversmith sits in front of the fire the entire time the silver is being refined and removes it only when he is able to see his own reflection in the flames. *Like the silversmith who watches over his silver, God always has His eyes on you and will continually watch*

over you while you are being refined. He is committed to you until the refining process of your grief journey is complete.

Once your deep wounds are healed, others will begin to see more of the reflection of Jesus Christ in your life. Instead of seeing a hurting, wounded individual, others will see a mature, seasoned, compassionate person, " . . . a vessel unto honor, sanctified, and meet for the master's use, and prepared unto every good work." (2 Timothy 2:21)

ONION APPROACH

The Lord may decide to take what I call the "onion approach," peeling back one or two layers of grief at a time. These layers of grief may not originate strictly from your present loss but from past losses in your life that have never been dealt with or processed. Losses that have never been grieved and processed will affect every aspect of your life. People who are hurting may not realize that their problems will usually always point back to a significant loss or hurt that was never grieved. There may be layers of losses that have never been grieved. If this has happened to you, you may be reading this book because it is *your time to heal.*

CHARACTER VS COMFORT

In my life, I have found that the Lord will work on only one or two areas of my Christian walk in a particular season. If God worked on all of your issues in the same season, you may become overwhelmed or give up altogether. It would be too much for one person to handle all at once.

Instead, He works little by little as you give Him permission, and as you cooperate with the dealings of the Holy Spirit in your life. Usually this will not only be a healing time but also a character building time.

The Lord will choose different seasons to teach you different principles in His Word or to bring you a personal truth or revelation that will enable you to walk in more freedom and victory in your everyday life.

When the Lord heals a layer of grief, His ultimate desire is to heal everything in you that hurts. His desire is to continually transform you more and more into the image of His dear Son, according to Romans 8:29.

Our job is twofold: to understand what God is purposing to teach us in each season of life, and to continually yield to the deeper work of the Holy Spirit.

PRAYER MINISTRY

There are special people within the body of Christ who are anointed and ordained of God to minister inner healing to the deep wounds of your past. Do not be afraid or embarrassed to seek out personal ministry when you are hurting. God will never embarrass you. He wants to heal you and set you free from grief.

Choosing someone skilled and anointed, yet someone you can trust, and someone who knows how to be discreet is very important. However, stay open to God. He may lead you to someone whom you may not have chosen for yourself.

Also, do not rule out what God can do in your heart during time spent alone with Him.

PERSONAL VISION

A vision came to me one day during my prayer time. I pictured Jesus and me by the Sea of Galilee. Jesus was sitting on a rock, and I was kneeling in front of Him with my head down on his lap. While clutching His folded hands tightly together under mine, the side of my face was pressed into His hands. I clung desperately to Jesus that day.

I felt safe with Jesus, but I also felt the need to talk. Crying, but not saying anything, I knew that He was aware of every painful situation in my life that I was describing to Him with my tears.

After a while, Jesus began to stand. Gently, He pulled His right hand from under mine—at first I tried to stop Him, but my hesitation to let go of His hand lasted for only seconds once I felt His loving, affirming touch on my head. The instant Jesus put His hand on my head I stopped crying. Once He touched me, I did not feel the need to say or speak anything more—a quietness and tranquil-like serenity enveloped me.

Then Jesus and I stood up and began walking along the water's edge. As we walked, He spoke not a word as every painful situation or loss that I had ever experienced flashed before me on what looked like a giant screen in the sky. As we walked silently together, I saw my daughter Stephanie, and instantly a great peace and release came over me.

All of the people that I cared so deeply about, and that were in my thoughts as I had cried my heart out to Jesus earlier that day flashed before me. These included my children, Richard and Candace, and my mother and father.

I knew that Jesus was reassuring me that even though I did not understand the loss of my daughter, not to view it as a failure because things are not always what they seem. I must trust Him. Jesus was lovingly asking me to trust Him with all the relationships and the people that I had been grieving deeply about in my heart and had been carrying around as a heavy burden. The Bible says that His yoke is easy and His burden is light (Matthew 11:30).

Even the relationships that I considered to be failures or losses, Jesus gave me peace about them. Just being with Him, the need to question things disappeared. As we continued to walk in silence, I knew in my heart that even though I did not understand why things had happened the way they did, I could still trust Jesus with it all.

We walked for a long time beside the sea—it was such a beautiful day—the sun was glistening on the water, butterflies were fluttering along, and birds were flying and chirping, making their own sweet music. All of creation was responding to the Creator.

As we turned to go back, Jesus gestured with his hand for me to look at the beauty of the flowers, and trees, and water, as far as my eyes could see. He motioned as if to say, *Look again my child, not at your past, but look at this beauty. Look at what is before you, for everything you see is all for your enjoyment. Even the fullness and beauty of the earth is for you to behold, to treasure, and to enjoy.*

I knew that Jesus was telling me not to dwell on things that made me feel sad, things that grieved my heart, but to look at the beauty of life all around. Jesus was telling me to take a second look—it was time to enjoy life once more.

All of a sudden, I began running through the thick, luscious, green grass so beautifully arrayed with tiny, white flowers. These little flowers were everywhere—they looked like a whole field of tiny baby's breath. As I ran, I bent down just a little so I could put my arms out to feel the touch of the grass and the beautiful flowers. Then suddenly, I began to leap and shout, "Yes! Yes!" As I shouted and continued to run, it released a joy, lightness, and freedom inside of me that I had known as a child but had since forgotten.

I was feeling like a little child again—untainted and full of life, joy, intrigue, wonder, expectation, and expression. It felt so right. I ran and jumped and leaped in the field, and then I looked over at Jesus. He was laughing and smiling.

This great joy that I was experiencing was also bringing great joy to Him.

I knew that Jesus would help me recapture this part of my life again. Jesus said, ". . . Except ye be converted, and become as little children, ye shall not enter into the kingdom of heaven" (Matthew 18:3). My heart yearned for the freedom and innocence that I had known as a child.

Then I ran as fast as I could and jumped into the water! The water felt so good—so refreshing and inviting! I splashed around shouting, "Yes! Yes!" I was enjoying myself so much, but I was still very aware that Jesus was with me, watching over me. Somehow I knew that He was pleased with me. It made me feel good inside. It made me feel pure and safe and wanted. I continued to splash around in the water, savoring my time with Jesus.

Jesus never took His eyes off of me. Then I got out of the water and ran toward Him, smiling into His face, enjoying the look of love that He had in His eyes for me. I knew that Jesus was reassuring me that no matter what happened, He would always love me and I would always hold a place dear in His heart. Oh, how wonderful it was to feel His love for me.

Then we walked some more along the sea. Jesus spoke to me without words; however, somehow I knew what he was saying to me. Now it was different—this time I did not want to speak. Words were not necessary. I just wanted to be with Jesus, to hear Him, to walk with Him, to listen to Him, to hear His heartbeat.

Jesus said for me to become like a little child. He said that when I was a child, I enjoyed dancing and playing. My life brought great joy to Him. He wanted this part of me to be expressed again. All I could think of was how much I wanted to be with Jesus and how much I wanted to please Him.

Great peace and comfort filled my heart that day as I visualized Jesus and me walking along the Sea of Galilee. Anytime I read my journal entry about this experience that I shared with Jesus, a renewed sense of peace and comfort comes over me. Just being in His presence is healing in itself.

COMFORT AND HEALING

This experience in prayer will forever be etched in my heart, and I will never forget how God used it to bring comfort and a sense of total well-being into my life that day.

This one experience with Him brought another level of healing to the deepest need of my heart. What does visualizing Jesus in the scene of a past hurtful event have to do with grieving?

The trauma of losing a loved one instills negative images into our subconscious that are automatically rehearsed over and over again in your mind, leaving you a victim of emotional pain, and sometimes leaving you in a constant state of emotional turmoil. Visualizing Jesus in the scene of those painful memories helps to remove the sting, the pain, and the trauma that is trapped within your emotions and your heart. Jesus is a healing balm.

REMOVE SCARS

Emotional healing will not erase your memory of things that have happened to you, but it will remove the painful emotions attached to the memory. According to inner healing expert, Ruth Carter Stapelton, in her book, *The Gift of Inner Healing,* "Some areas of our lives can only be healed by the power of the Holy Spirit. Only the Holy Spirit can move back into these areas and remove the scars."[2]

Some people have asked, *"When will I know that I have been healed from the wounds of my past?"* You will know that healing has occurred when you are no longer upset about your past or your loss, and when the events of your past have been completely resolved and laid to rest in your mind and in your heart. When you reach this place on the inside, you have made peace with your past.

THE GREAT PHYSICIAN

While you are grieving, you will be under the care of the Great Physician, who will meticulously guide you through the different stages of recovery. If you do not follow your Doctor's advice, you could suffer a relapse. Your diagnosis is emotional trauma brought on by a tragic loss.

PROGNOSIS, PATHWAY, PRESCRIPTION

Your prognosis is excellent, and it comes out of Psalm 118:17, which says, "I shall not die, but live, and declare the works of the LORD." Your spiritual prescription is spending more time in prayer and in the presence of God.

Follow the advice of the Great Physician; trust the pathway and prescription that He gives you for your emotional healing. Expect setbacks and maybe even some extended time in recovery. But give yourself the space needed to create a new beginning customized by God with you in mind.

SUMMING IT UP

When is your healing complete? When there is no more crying, no more inappropriate anger, no more sorrow, no more heartache, no more acting out, no more issues, no more bitterness, no more pain, and no more walls. Then you can truly sing, *"Bless the Lord, oh my soul and all that is within me bless His holy name, FOR I AM HEALED!"*

Bless the LORD, O my soul: and all that is within me, bless his holy name. Bless the LORD, O my soul, and forget not all his benefits: Who forgiveth all thine iniquities; who healeth all thy diseases; Who redeemeth thy life from destruction; who crowneth thee with lovingkindness and tender mercies; Who satisfieth thy mouth with good things; so that thy youth is renewed like the eagle's. (Psalm 103:1-5)

The following is a list of practical suggestions to help you find help for the first time or as you continue on your healing journey:

- Seek out prayer ministries that I have mentioned in the resource section of this book.
- Pastoral counseling/prayer
- Godly counsel/prayer from a more mature Christian
- Getting real with a godly friend with whom you can share (he or she may need reciprocal prayer) and be accountable. This is how it happened for me.
- Realize that your healing journey may take years as God refines you. Do not expect overnight deliverance for all of your issues.
- Do a personal bible study, looking for all the verses you can find about inner healing, cleansing, deliverance, freedom, etc. God will use His Word to reach "the inner parts" and help you individually.

Inner Healing Prayer

Dear Heavenly Father,

Search me, O God, and know my heart: try me and know my thoughts: And see if there be any wicked way in me, and lead me in the way everlasting (Psalm 139:23-24).

Holy Spirit, I welcome you into my life. As you search my heart, show me what is keeping me from being the person you want me to be—show me what is keeping me from healing.

I ask You Lord to heal me of past hurts—heal the wounds that have kept me in bondage. Help me to face my past and let go of this _____ (specific hurts). Forgive me for holding on to these hurts—take away the painful memories that linger in my mind. Take away the power they have over me.

I forgive _____ for the hurts they caused in my life. I release them from any debt I thought they owed me and I put them now into Your hands. I release all hurts, all offenses, all of my anger to you, Lord.

And I repent of _____; please forgive me of this offense, Lord. Thank You for cleansing my heart from all unrighteousness.

Jesus, come into my heart. Let me see You in every hurt of my life. I want to hear Your voice and feel Your touch. Give me the freedom and peace I so yearn for. I close my eyes now—I am picturing You, Jesus, sitting on a rock along the water's edge. Take me with You, Jesus, as you walk along the Sea of Galilee. Show me beautiful things from the works of Your Hands.

Fill me today with Your joy, Your peace, and Your love, Lord Jesus. I love you with all my heart. I surrender my all to You and I receive Your healing touch today, in Jesus' name. Amen.

JOURNAL NOTES

Chapter Six

FORGIVING ALL

And be ye kind one to another, tenderhearted, forgiving one another, even as God for Christ's sake hath forgiven you.   Ephesians 4:32

Once you have spent time processing your grief emotions, an important next step to full recovery has to do with being able to forgive. Most experts agree that forgiveness is a major key to grief recovery, but it can be one of the last and most difficult areas to overcome. Complete emotional healing will not take place until you are walking in a place of total forgiveness, continually guarding your heart against anger, offense, and bitterness, while at the same time keeping it pure, tender, and humble before God.

Forgiveness is not a one-time event but a process. The process takes time, but genuine forgiveness will free you from the pain and unpleasant memories of the past and will help to heal the wounded emotions that emerge after you experience a tragic loss. As stated before, loss will always create a certain amount of emotional pain that will in turn, bring to the surface, issues from your past that need to be resolved. You may not be aware of your issues, but God has a way of bringing them to the surface when it is *your time to heal*.

What is forgiveness? According to Webster's Dictionary, *forgiveness* means to "*give up resentment, to pardon, to absolve, to grant relief from payment, or to allow room for error or weakness.*"[1] The word forgiveness occurs more than 140 times in the New Testament, demonstrating its utmost importance in the life of a believer.

My healing required that I worked on resolving the issues of anger and unforgiveness in my heart. This meant that every time I became upset, I had to repent for being angry, and then I had to forgive the person with whom I was angry. Hebrews 12:1 tells us to "lay aside every weight, and the sin which doth so easily beset us, and let us run with patience the race that is set before us." In his book, *Neither Give Place*, author Jefferson H. Floyd expounds on this scripture in Hebrews 12 by saying:

> This passage defines two primary events that a person who wants to be free should go through in his life: laying aside every weight (giving forgiveness) and being unshackled from besetting sin (confes-

sion of sin). One gets free from bitterness by giving forgiveness and gets free from the contamination of past sins by getting forgiveness.[2]

My experience had more to do with forgiving than being forgiven. Releasing forgiveness became an important part of my healing journey—even when the recipient was Almighty God.

ANGRY WITH GOD

Did I really have anger toward God? No way! Never! I love God. One day, however, I went to see a couple to receive prayer ministry and the first question they asked me after hearing my story was, "Are you angry with God?" I thought to myself, how *dare this couple ask me that question. They know that as a minister, I would know better than to have unforgiveness in my heart toward God. God and I are okay. Why is this couple making such a big deal about this?*

"Of course not!" I blurted out, somewhat defensively. "I came here to get prayed for about losing my daughter." Ignoring what I said, they asked me to read a prayer typed out on a piece of paper. When I looked down at the paper, the heading read, "Anger/Disappointment with God Prayer." (See the end of this chapter for a copy of this prayer.) Having to respond to the question of whether or not I was angry with God was actually making me angry. By now, I was determined to read the prayer just to prove them wrong.

The minute I began reading, something unexpected happened. I could not speak. My vocal cords refused to cooperate with my mouth, which caused a physical chain reaction of choking and coughing. That simple question had evoked an unexpected response in me, and all of a sudden, I began crying from the depths of my soul.

Until this time, I had not been able to identify my true feelings, or understand why I was so angry all the time. But they were right. This couple had discerned the root of my problem and confronted me with truth.

Being angry with God was not something that I had to make a conscious decision about, but negative feelings had entered my heart through the emotional trauma of losing my daughter. In addition to that, I still had suppressed anger issues over hurts from my childhood that I had never resolved. Because I never took the time to face these issues, it only made matters worse. Going for prayer ministry forced me to open my heart to God and get in touch with my true feelings.

The anger I had at God was coming from my emotions and not from my heart, because in my heart I loved God and I knew that God loved me. My anger at God was an emotional response stemming from the loss of my daughter. Deep down inside I knew that I could not blame Him. What happened to Stephanie was not God's fault.

EMOTIONAL BAGGAGE

As time went on, more and more emotional baggage surfaced. Feelings of abandonment and punishment topped the list. I felt that God had failed me. I had believed for Stephanie's healing but it had not come to pass. I felt that God had allowed my daughter to die without the slightest consideration of how it might destroy me in the process. I felt that Stephanie had been taken from me in the most unjust and unfair way. Nothing in my life made sense anymore. My world had been turned upside down.

Could it be that you are angry with God? How do you resolve anger and unforgiveness toward an Almighty, Righteous God? Because it has been so ingrained in Christians that you cannot be angry with God, there may be a tendency to suppress your true feelings when in reality, you might actually feel intense anger toward God.

If you want to be healed, though, you must be willing to search your heart and be honest about how you feel. Honesty is the only thing that works because honesty gives God permission to help you. And honesty takes you out of the land of denial.

Because God already knows what is inside your heart, confess to Him how you really feel. Instead of pretending to be okay, which is what I did, learn how to express your true feelings. Tell Him how much your loss devastated you. Tell Him how sometimes you are angry at everything and everyone.

Get it out of your system by saying it, praying it, or writing it down. King David writes in Psalm 62:8 (NIV) to, "Trust in him at all times, O people; pour out your hearts to him, for God is our refuge. Selah." *Being honest about how you feel removes the power that painful emotions can have over you. This is another healthy way to process your grief and move forward in your healing journey.*

ANGER TOWARD SELF

The other person I was angry with was myself. As difficult as it was to admit, I blamed myself for not waking up and being able to help my daughter the night she died. Even though I did not sense her emergency, I felt that as her mother, I should have instinctively known that something was wrong and therefore, should have been able to help her. I was angry because of my inability to respond to her struggle that night, and it was actually easier to forgive God than it was to forgive myself.

Like me, some of you may feel responsible for your loss because there is no one else to blame or because you cannot find any other explanation. Healing will not come until you are able to release all of your anger and guilt through the simple act of forgiving yourself. Give yourself a break and let yourself off the hook. God has.

Releasing the anger in my heart took time, but I knew that I would have to let go of blaming myself and feeling responsible for my daughter's death in order to heal. I also knew that my daughter would not want me to blame myself for her death. As I cried out to God, asking Him to lift this heavy burden, He brought me to a place where I could finally extend to myself the gift of forgiveness and mercy that I would have extended to anyone else in my shoes.

Author Earl Hipp writes in his book, *Help for the Hard Times,*

" . . . A very important person to forgive is yourself. You can forgive yourself for all the things you didn't do, or say or become. Maybe you feel bad about how you treated people before or after the loss, how you expressed your anger or frustration, or how you didn't think to say, "I love you." In grief, as in life, everyone always does the best they can and still no one manages to do it perfectly. Everyone deserves forgiveness, and that includes you."[3]

NO STRANGER TO LOSS

As I looked back over my life after Stephanie's death, I realized that I was no stranger to loss. Ten years earlier, I had experienced a bitter divorce that involved my second daughter, Candace. My husband wanted a divorce and the custody of our daughter. After hearing the testimonies and deliberating our case, the jurors decided that Candace should live with her father. I was totally taken aback by their decision, never thinking for one moment that the court would take a child from his or her biological mother. But I was wrong. In one day, my marriage ended in divorce, and I lost custody of my 10-year-old daughter. That day was one of the worst days of my life.

Once the decision of the jurors was read, I remember the immediate hatred I had in my heart toward them, staring into each of their eyes as if to say, *"How could you!"* My contempt for the defense attorney representing Candace's father gripped my heart with stone coldness.

When I left the courtroom that day, I left speechless, broken, and publicly shamed. Twelve people had decided that Candace's father was the better parent of the two of us. In doing so, they had indirectly labeled me as an unfit mother.

On the outside I looked calm, but on the inside I was totally crushed and blown away by what happened. Mixed feelings of anger, hatred, unforgiveness, pain, heartache, doubts, fears, shame, guilt, embarrassment, condemnation, and offense followed me home that day.

I could not believe the predicament I was in, although I hoped that at any moment, someone would wake me up and tell me it was all a bad dream. It was not a dream, however, and the reality and consequences of what happened that day would affect my life for many years to follow.

On a spiritual level, I did not realize that my agreement with negative thoughts and emotions during my marriage separation created a legal ground for unforgiveness and bitterness to settle in and take root in my heart. Within a twelve-month period, I had lost my daughter, my marriage, my family, and my home. My whole life was unraveling before my very eyes.

At that point, the only thing I knew to do was fall on my face before God and cry out for His mercy. The truth, which was difficult to realize but needed to be accepted, was that I could not blame God or anyone else for what happened.

Candace's father and I had been separated for nearly three years when our divorce was finalized. After a few years of standing and praying for my marriage to be healed, of watching and waiting, of being alone and not seeing one glimmer of hope in getting back together, I became weary in well-doing and decided to live life my way. It was during this time of doing things my way that the enemy came in to steal, kill, and destroy. (See John 10:10.)

When bad things occur and you're trying to find answers, you should first pray to see if there is any sin in your life. If sin is your problem, you must be willing to humble yourself and repent before God. If being out of the will of God in any area of your life is not the issue, then you can confidently stand on the Word of God with all of Heaven backing you in a warfare position against the enemy. However, if you have any area of compromise in your life, as I had, you must repent and ask the Lord to forgive you.

We know from Psalm 51 that David had to deal with a past that he would rather have chosen to ignore. Maybe your emotional baggage is not quite as great as his or even mine, but there is much to be learned from his confession. Part of it I include here for you to consider:

> Cleanse me with hyssop, and I will be clean;
> > wash me, and I will be whiter than snow.
> Let me hear joy and gladness;
> > let the bones you have crushed rejoice.
> Hide your face from my sins
> > and blot out all my iniquity.
> Create in me a pure heart, O God,
> > and renew a steadfast spirit within me.
> Do not cast me from your presence
> > or take your Holy Spirit from me.
> Restore to me the joy of your salvation
> > and grant me a willing spirit, to sustain me.

Psalms 51:7-12 (NIV)

Eventually, all the negative feelings associated with my divorce and custody battle were resolved, but it took many years of praying, obeying and studying God's Word to renew my mind. I also had to repent where needed and forgive the people I had bitterness towards in my heart. I had to work on keeping my heart and mind free of negative emotions and thoughts.

It took time to sort through the many issues surrounding my divorce and to forgive, but somewhere along the pathway of obedience, I was finally able to see my losses, failures, sin, and other people through God's eyes and with His heart.

The act of humbling yourself before God and being able to forgive others is something that you will need to do over and over again. Why? Because we live in a fallen world and hurting people, hurt people. This is a small price to pay for staying free and pleasing God.

LET IT GO

The decision to let go of anger and unforgiveness played a significant role in my ability to grieve my losses and move on with my life. Your love for God and your sincere desire to obey Him will make it difficult to live any other life than the one He has ordained for you. Jesus said in John 14:23, ". . . If anyone loves Me, he will keep My Word; and My Father will love him, and We will come to him and make Our abode with him." (NASB)

Losing custody of my daughter Candace and accepting the failure of my marriage required God's grace, as well as time with my face continually before the Lord. I wish I could tell you that I was able to forgive my former husband the first night I returned home without my daughter by my side. I could not, because I was too devastated and angry.

I wish I could tell you that since that time, I have never had a problem with anger and unforgiveness, but that would not be true. I wish I could tell you that I have never since had a problem with shame or any other negative emotion, but that would only be pretense.

Just like everyone else, I had to choose how I would handle the hurtful things that came into my life. How you respond to what happens to you will not only determine your outlook on life, but your outcome in life as well. Remember that it is not what happens *to you* but *in you* that matters. The type of person you become in the wake of your loss will tell your story more than anything else.

The question to ask yourself is this: "Will you emerge victorious in life in spite of your loss or will you give up and throw in the towel? Will you continue to believe in God's goodness or will you misjudge God in the midst of your pain?"

HIS PATHWAY

God had a pathway of restoration and healing mapped out for me—a pathway in which I was about to embark. He led me to a ministry that spoke often on the power of forgiveness, healing, and restoration in marriages and relationships.

Ironically, part of my prescription for healing came through many years of interceding and standing in the gap for the very people who had hurt and wounded me in the past. If you are praying earnestly for someone, it can begin the process of healing a hardened heart.

Prayer tenderizes your heart and endears you toward the people you uphold before God in prayer. A tender heart is one that is willing to forgive and let go of the most grievous offense. A tenderhearted person is one who is willing to say, "I'm sorry . . . I was wrong." A tenderhearted person is one who is willing to ask the question that no one else may be asking. The question is: "Will you please forgive me?"

BELIEVING GOD

Believing what God said about me in His Word began to remove deep feelings of shame and guilt, which in turn, helped me to love and accept myself more. I realized that if God could forgive me, I could forgive myself. When you go through difficulties, you are not without hope, because God is always there to pick up the pieces of your life and restore the years of mistakes and heartaches. His promise of restoration in Joel 2:25-27 (NKJV) states,

> So I will restore to you the years that the swarming locust has eaten, the crawling locust, the consuming locust, and the chewing locust . . . Then you shall know that I am in the midst of Israel: I am the LORD your God and there is no other. My people shall never be put to shame.

Remember that forgiveness will open a spiritual door through which God is able to begin His restoration process in your life. Like forgiveness, restoration is a process, but as you purpose in your heart to walk upright before God, He will make all things beautiful in His time, and complete the process of healing in your life.

THE RIGHT PERSPECTIVE

Someone once made a comment to me that I have never forgotten. He said, "You don't have a problem Doris, you just need the right perspective." Perspective has to do with how you see things. With the right perspective, you can overcome any problem in life. Whenever the enemy reminds you of your losses, choose to believe the Word of God over your circumstances.

Refuse to accept the voice of defeat. In order to do this, the Word of God must have the final say in your life. Your experiences do not change the written Word, but the Word of God abiding in you can change your reactions to them.

When those old feelings of guilt, condemnation, and unforgiveness try to resurface and control you, instead of succumbing to them, release everything in your life (the good, the bad, the ugly, the victories, the losses, the failures, the successes) to the Lordship of Jesus Christ.

Then work on maintaining your perspective. Why? Because we are all like sheep that have gone astray; we have all made mistakes; we all need help; we all need love; we all need mercy; and we all need forgiveness. With God's help you can forgive anyone, you can live again, you can love again, you can let go, you can overcome the pain of loss, you can dream again, and you can be healed!

MAKE PEACE WITH YOUR PAST

During my journey to healing I realized that I had never grieved the pain of my past. When Stephanie died, it only compounded and complicated my grief. Hidden shame over losing custody of my daughter had remained in my life from years past in an almost secretive way. I never talked about the custody battle because I always felt that if I shared what happened, others would think less of me or judge me; therefore, I kept all these feelings of shame locked away in a secret compartment in my heart.

Any place of secrecy in your life will be an entry point where the enemy can snare your walk with God, or at the least, continue to torment your mind over past mistakes and failures.

The trauma of Stephanie's death opened this hidden wound where all the old debris of the past had laid dormant for many years. As the old wounds surfaced, I had to deal with them—I had to grieve the old losses and unresolved hurts, along with the new pain of loss. I had to make peace with my past in order to find closure with Stephanie's death.

THE FRUIT OF FORGIVENESS

Several years ago I heard about a pastor whose son was murdered. The man who brutally murdered his son was apprehended and sentenced to life in prison. The pastor struggled with hatred toward this man, but one day he decided that unforgiveness and bitterness would not rule his life. He started praying on a regular basis for the man who had murdered his son. Then the Lord prompted him to go to the prison to visit and befriend his son's killer. Over time, the pastor was able to forgive him completely and has since embraced this man as a surrogate son. Most importantly, this pastor was also used by God to lead the man who murdered his son to the Lord. What a great testimony of two lives that were forever changed because someone was willing to *forgive all*.

KEYS TO VICTORY:

1. **Repenting and releasing forgiveness from your heart are important because healing is impossible if forgiveness is not present.** Being unrepentant will keep the wounds alive and the hurt attached to you.

2. **True forgiveness is always preceded by true repentance.** For example, someone may have legitimately wronged you, but if you judged him or her in the process, before you can truly forgive him or her, you will first need to repent of all judgments you made in your heart against him or her. Jesus taught us in the Beatitudes to stop pointing the finger at others but instead, to look first within ourselves to our own areas of weakness. Matthew 7:3 states, "And why beholdest

thou the mote that is in thy brother's eye, but considerest not the beam that is in thine own eye?"
3. **Practicing repentance and forgiveness will keep your heart tender and open to Jesus.** In Revelation 3:20, Jesus said, "Behold, I stand at the door, and knock: if any man hear my voice, and open the door, I will come in to him, and will sup with him, and he with me." Continue to stay sensitive to His knock. Jesus wants to spend time with you over your loss. He wants to speak words of life to you.

IT'S A CHOICE

Is there someone in your life that you need to forgive? Do you need to ask someone else for forgiveness? Do you need to forgive yourself? Forgiveness begins with a decision. Forgiveness is a choice that each individual makes in order to let go of an offense, no matter how grievous it may have been. As mentioned earlier in this chapter, this includes forgiving yourself if necessary.

You do not have control over the actions of others, but you do have control over what you allow in your heart, what you say, and what you do. If you are waiting on the reactions of others to decide if you will forgive, it may never happen on your timetable. The key is to determine in your heart beforehand that no matter what the other person does or says, you will forgive as an act of your will and in obedience to God. Do this before the altercation happens.

LEVELS OF FORGIVENESS

When you are unable to forgive, it should be a sign that there is an area in your life that you have not given over to God. Perhaps there was a situation in which you thought you forgave someone but, when placed in the right set of circumstances, you realized that there was still a tinge of unforgiveness in your heart.

Could it be that you only forgave at the surface level and not at the deepest level? *The deepest level of forgiveness comes from the heart. A wounded heart is healed when you forgive at the deepest level, and that is why it is so important to not harbor unforgiveness while you are grieving.* True forgiveness has the power to heal relationships, because once your heart is healed, the emotional wounds that kept you estranged from others are now removed. Communication can be restored. Love can be restored. Lives can be changed. Relationships can be healed.

As I was progressing through grief, the Lord began to heal my relationship with my daughter, Candace. We grew much closer together after Stephanie's death. Our relationship was strained and distant before, but now it was time to lay down our differences and let the healing begin—to reach some common ground—to agree to disagree and to forgive each other for hurtful things we had said to each other in the past. Grieving does not have to be a negative experience, but you can use this time to focus on healing and reconciliation in relationships where it is needed.

BEFORE THE SUN GOES DOWN

The Bible says to forgive an offense before the sun goes down. Ephesians 4:26 states, "Be ye angry, and sin not: let not the sun go down upon your wrath:" In other words, do not go to sleep with anger and unforgiveness in your heart. The best way to keep from going to bed angry is to make a decision ahead of time that you will forgive no matter what the circumstances are. Once any offense occurs, the key is to immediately release forgiveness from your heart.

Forgiving at the heart level is when you release all judgments, blame, guilt, and accusations toward the person who hurt you and in return, you feel no pain or hurt toward them. Let this criteria determine whether or not you have truly forgiven someone.

IT'S A GIFT

When you forgive at this level, you have given the most unselfish gift that anyone could give—you have given the gift of forgiveness. Remember that a gift is something you choose to give freely—it is not something you are forced to give. God's heart is one that gives freely and His heart abides within the heart of every believer. Through His grace you can forgive and let go of any offense or hurt. When you cannot think of any reason in the natural to forgive, do it for God. Forgive on God's behalf. Forgive on His account and for His benefit. He's worth it! Romans 8:32 states, "He that spared not his own Son, but delivered him up for us all, how shall he not with him also freely give us all things?"

BITTERNESS

If you do not forgive, you will risk becoming a critical and bitter person, never growing past your emotional wounds — never healing from your loss, or never experiencing healing in relationships with others. Bitterness is like a cancer that eats away at your soul and poisons you and everyone else around you.

You can always locate a bitter person by the words they speak. They may get an immediate adrenaline rush and the attention of others by hating and placing blame. However, though you get attention at first, others quickly tire of hearing you.

The effects of bitterness are far-reaching, with the ability to destroy minds, lives, and human relationships. The Bible warns us to diligently guard, protect, and give attention to this area of our lives. Hebrews 12:14-15 states, "Follow peace with all men, and holiness, without which no man shall see the Lord: Looking diligently lest any man fail of the grace of God; lest any root of bitterness springing up trouble you, and thereby many be defiled."

One example of someone who fell into the trap of bitterness, blame and unforgiveness happened to a family member of a friend of mine. The tragedy hit her brother-in-law's family. His college-age daughter was at Baylor, and one day she was driving by the campus and was hit by a drunk driver running a light. She was killed in the crash. That was about 15 years ago, and to this day the deceased girl's mother is still bitter and unforgiving. She distinctly said to my friend that she was mad at God. And even thou she won a hefty lawsuit against the other driver, money can never make up for the loss of her daughter or the bitterness that unforgiveness brought into her life.

DEFILEMENT

Unresolved bitterness will always lead to *defilement*. Defilement in Webster's Dictionary means *"to make filthy or dirty, to corrupt."*[4] Once you have been defiled, the only antidote is forgiveness. If you are having a difficult time forgiving someone, pray and ask God for more grace to forgive. If you are really serious about forgiving, God will empower you by His grace to forgive for good.

The worst legacy you could leave your deceased loved one is to become bitter after he or she dies. You can choose to bring honor and meaning to your loss or you can bring dishonor and shame to the memory of your deceased loved ones—all by how you handle their loss and what type of person you ultimately become in the twilight of their death. This saying holds true for any type of loss.

CLEANSING

Webster's Dictionary defines *clean* as *"free from dirt or disease, pure, and honorable."*[5] As you confess your sins, a spiritual cleansing takes place in your heart. Neglecting to clean a physical wound with peroxide or some type of antiseptic could cause the wound to become seriously infected. Likewise, without cleaning your emotional wounds with the antiseptic of repentance and forgiveness, your heart could become seriously infected, with the possibility of bitterness spreading to other areas of your life. Cleansing is always necessary before complete healing can occur.

NO BAGGAGE

Another important aspect to remember about forgiveness is what happens when you do not forgive others. You actually bind that person to yourself spiritually. When you bind someone to you, all of that person's baggage comes along for the ride. But when you forgive them, you release them from you, including their baggage. John 20:23 says, "Whosoever sins ye remit, they are remitted unto them; and whosoever sins ye retain, they are retained."

WHY FORGIVE?

Why should you forgive? When you decide to forgive someone who has hurt you, it pleases Jesus. Because He told you to forgive, it is the right thing to do. Forgiveness is the one thing that will keep walls of offense from developing between you and another person. When you forgive others with no strings attached, it gives God room to deal with the other person—in His way and in His timing. The Bible says in Proverbs 25:21-22, "If thine enemy be hungry, give him bread to eat; and if he be thirsty, give him water to drink: For thou shalt heap coals of fire upon his head, and the LORD shall reward thee."

Another reason to consider is that when you have sown seeds of forgiveness, those seeds will be available to you when you need someone else to forgive you. Luke 6:38 states, ". . . for with the same measure that ye mete withal it shall be measured to you again." Keep forgiveness in your storehouse—it will be there when you need it most.

SUMMING IT UP

Forgiveness is an important issue for anyone who has been traumatized by loss. Understandably, emotions run high during the grieving process, issues from your past resurface, and hearts struggle with fresh wounds from the pain of loss. As for me, I did not realize that I had anger and unforgiveness in my life until the Lord revealed what was in my heart during a prayer ministry time. I did not realize that old hurts from my past had to be resolved and released before acceptance and closure could come. Now I know that forgiveness is a prerequisite to healing.

When you understand how important forgiveness becomes in your healing journey, you will find the courage to face your darkest feelings. You will do whatever it takes to remove all anger and unforgiveness from your heart. With God's help, you can forgive anyone, even if it means forgiving yourself.

One of the most important keys to being healed from loss and grief is to continually forgive, forgive, and again I say, *forgive!*

FORGIVENESS PRAYERS

Anger/Disappointment with God

Dear Lord, I see that I have misjudged you and blamed you for things that you did not do. I choose to stop doing this. I ask you to forgive me for my sin against you. I know and affirm that you are a good God and that you want only the best for me, which is to transform me into the image of Jesus Christ.

I agree with you that you are in charge of my life, and that everything that happens to me is for my development and maturing into a son/daughter, able to rule and reign with you in eternity.

I will put the blame where it really belongs, on myself and on Satan. I will stop being a blame shifter, but will be responsible for my own life, under the guidance and control of the Holy Spirit.

Thank you, Lord, for new freedom today, and for a renewed relationship with you. I receive both of these in the name of Jesus Christ. Amen!

Forgiving Others

Father, you have made it clear that you require me to forgive. You desire the healing and freedom for me that forgiveness brings. So today, I choose to forgive all who have set me up to enter into sin and all who have hurt me. I choose to release them, each and every one. I let go of all judgments against them, and I let go of all punishments for them that I have harbored in my heart. I turn all of this, and all of them, over to you.

Holy Spirit, I thank you for working forgiveness into my life, for giving me the grace I need to forgive, and for continuing to enable me to forgive. In Jesus' name, Amen!

Asking God's Forgiveness

Father, now that I have forgiven all others, I thank you that I can now come to receive your forgiveness. So I come to you, through the shed blood of Jesus and the power of His Cross, asking you to forgive me of all of my sins. I acknowledge and take responsibility for each and every time I have violated your commandments, as well as for the iniquity that is in my heart.

Holy Spirit, thank you for working forgiveness into my life, for healing me, and for cleansing me from all unrighteousness. Thank You, Father, for restoring me to fellowship with you. In the name of Jesus Christ, I pray. Amen!

Forgiving Myself

Father, because you have forgiven me, I choose to forgive myself and to release myself from all accusations, judgments, hatred, slander, mistakes, stupidity, and falling short of the mark. I choose to accept myself just as I am because you accept me. I choose to love myself because you love me. I expect to begin to like myself.

Holy Spirit, I ask you, I give you permission, and I expect you to work your work of sanctification in me. I fully embrace this truth and look forward to working with you so I can be changed into the image of Christ.

In the name of Jesus Christ I pray. Amen!

*Forgiveness Prayers taken from *Restoring the Foundations*
Copyright 2001, Proclaiming His Word, Inc.

JOURNAL NOTES

Chapter Seven

TRUSTING GOD

I will sing of the mercies of the LORD forever; with my mouth will I make known thy faithfulness to all generations. Psalm 89:1

LAUREN'S LIFE

As shown in this next heart wrenching loss, surviving any tragedy demands that you place your faith and trust in a higher power. Lauren and her husband were supposed to visit her parents later that day, but after not arriving at their house as planned, and after several hours of not being able to reach his daughter, Damon decided to ride over to his daughter's home to check on them.

What he found was horrifying! His daughter had been murdered, and apparently his son-in-law had turned the gun on himself and committed suicide. At the memorial service, one of the ministers named Matt made this profound statement:

> I know that in this tragedy we have all asked the question of why? Why would this happen to Lauren and why would this happen to this family? But God has helped me understand that there is no answer for our heads that will satisfy the pain in our heart. Let us not seek an answer, which cannot be given—let us see our heavenly Father who wants to hold us in His arms.

Can you imagine how reassuring and comforting those words must have been to this young woman's family and friends that day. This compassionate minister was able to set the tone for the entire memorial service by turning their focus away from the pain of what happened to focusing on God's heart for each of them, and the precious life of a beautiful young woman named Lauren.

RELATIONSHIP

When you have experienced a personal loss of this magnitude, the one relationship you must hold on to with every ounce of your strength is your relationship with God. His love, His goodness, and His faithfulness will see you through a tragedy too horrendous for words to articulate, or for natural understanding to communicate. Psalm 89:24

states, "But my faithfulness and my mercy shall be with him: and in my name shall his horn be exalted." Your relationship with God is your foundation and source of strength in everything of this life.

When a tragic loss occurs, our tendency as human beings is to feel forsaken by God. But instead of feeling forsaken by God in your hour of darkness, you must run to God and release your faith toward the one and only true God who is forever faithful, and good, and whose mercies are new every morning. Lamentations 3:22-23 says, "It is of the LORD'S mercies that we are not consumed, because his compassions fail not. They are new every morning: great is thy faithfulness."

You may not recognize His faithfulness and goodness in the instant of your tragedy, but look for it in everything, because God will remain faithful to you in your darkest hour. He wants you to trust in His faithfulness and allow Him to help and comfort you in your hour of need.

Without faith you cannot please God, and without faith you cannot receive from God. But with faith, you can receive all that God has for you. By faith, you can receive complete healing from grief.

Hebrews 11:6 states, "But without faith it is impossible to please him: for he that cometh to God must believe that he is, and that he is a rewarder of them that diligently seek him." Maintaining your faith in God after you have experienced a tragic loss will be a key component to your peace, your confidence, your healing, and your emotional well-being. Your faith is your lifeline to God—faith keeps you connected to God.

NO BLAME

As mentioned in an earlier chapter, even when you have an intimate relationship with the Lord, the trauma of a tragic loss can cause you to question or blame God. Questions like, "How could God let this happen" or "Why did God do this?" are typical questions after a tragedy strikes.

Though you may never fully understand why this tragedy occurred, one thing you can be completely sure of is this—God is not to blame. It is not His fault. The Bible says that Jesus came to give life and life more abundantly and that Satan comes to steal, kill, and destroy. (See John 10:10.)

If blame must be placed, then it certainly should not be placed on God. Do not allow your lack of understanding, your confusion, and your deep pain to shift anger and blame toward God. However, if you have blamed God and you are angry with Him, simply forgive Him as you would anyone else.

Instead of blaming God, trust in His goodness and faithfulness. Lean to Him for support, and let Him wrap His loving arms around you to comfort you, heal you, and love you.

FAITHFUL DEFINED

The Greek definition for the word *faithful* means *"trustworthy, sure, and true."*[1] Webster's Dictionary defines *faithful* as *"unchanging in attachment to a person or cause; reliable; absence of change, and thus lack of fickleness."*[2] These definitions describe the character of God. When you reflect on His attributes, remember that He will be forever faithful to you.

UNCHANGING

When bad things happen, God does not expect you to deny your circumstances or the deep pain you feel in your heart. He wants you to trust Him in spite of your circumstances and in spite of how you feel. Like me, the magnitude of your loss may have shaken your faith to the core, but your tragedy has not changed God. He has not stopped being God—your God. You must still believe in His faithfulness and goodness toward you.

His faithfulness cannot be turned on and off like a faucet or light switch. He does not sway or fluctuate due to circumstances beyond His control. He is always in control for He is God of the universe. James 1:17 says that He is, " . . . the Father of lights, with whom is no variableness, neither shadow of turning."

When bad things happened in my life, it somehow made me feel unloved. But remember that God still loves you just as much now as when your life was conceived before the foundation of the world. Your tragic loss or unanswered prayer is not a sign that He is punishing you or that He is mad at you. The Bible says, "Jesus Christ the same yesterday, and today, and for ever." (Hebrews 13:8). His heart of love and faithfulness toward you will remain constant throughout your life. He will not break covenant with you for any reason because God is the original covenant keeper.

Do not allow suffering to cause your belief and trust in the goodness and faithfulness of God to waver. Without this basic trust in God, you have nothing to stand on and you have nothing to release your faith toward when life throws you a curve ball.

Everything else in your life will eventually become sinking sand without a basic trust and belief in God the Father. When the storms of life come, (and they will) He is your rock, your security, and your solid foundation.

> Therefore everyone who hears these words of mine and puts them into practice is like a wise man who built his house on the rock. The rain came down, the streams rose, and the winds blew and beat against that house; yet it did not fall, because it had its foundation on the rock. (Matthew 7:24-25 NIV)

RECALL HIS GOODNESS

The perfect time to recall all the wonderful ways that God has proven His faithfulness and goodness toward you is when you are hurting over a loss. Think of the all the times in the past that God worked things out for your good. Think of all the times God came through for you. Think of where you would be today if Romans 8:31 which says, "... If God be for us, who can be against us?" were not true.

When painful circumstances tried to overshadow and possibly steal King David's trust in the Lord, he quickly reminded himself of how good God had been to him throughout his lifetime. He turned to God as his source of comfort and strength. He inquired of the Lord for direction. He worshipped the Lord for intimacy. This would be David's way of handling trials and tribulations throughout his reign as king. He turned to God, not away from Him.

One example of King David's turning to God while he was grieving is when his illegitimate child with Bathsheba died. David wept and fasted around the clock while the child was ill, but once he found out that the child died, he worshipped God and ended his fast.

When his servants questioned his behavior, King David said, "... While the child was yet alive, I fasted and wept: for I said, who can tell whether GOD will be gracious to me, that the child may live? But now he is dead, wherefore should I fast? can I bring him back again? I shall go to him, but he shall not return to me" (2 Samuel 12:22-23).

Although David experienced a season of grief, he still chose to worship God, revealing his trust in the faithfulness of God. You can see in this passage that David did not disconnect from God because of tragedy, but he stayed connected to God through faith, trusting that God would continue to show mercy toward him as He has done in the past.

David believed in the sovereignty of God, therefore, after praying and fasting for his child, he chose to leave the final outcome of his child's life in God's hands.

TURN YOUR EYES

Just like King David, you must do more than grieve; you must turn your focus to God. Instead of focusing on the pain of your loss, turn your eyes toward Jesus. Some things are much too agonizing and gruesome for your mind to accept or comprehend. That is why it is important to keep your focus on what brings comfort and peace to your soul. Wrong thinking about the goodness and faithfulness of God does not produce the comfort and peace that belongs to you as a believer. Turning your focus to Jesus can be done with one quick decision. The benefit is affirmed in the following lyrics from the song, "Turn Your Eyes Upon Jesus"[3]:

Turn your eyes upon Jesus,
Look full in His wonderful face,
And the things of earth will grow strangely dim,
In the light of His glory and grace.

Looking into His wonderful face will mean that your entire heart, soul, and mind are totally focused on God the

Son, on His goodness, and on His love for you. As you turn your focus away from the pain of your loss, and as you turn your eyes toward Jesus, you will begin to see how much more peaceful your life will become.

Everything in your life will find its proper place when Jesus is given first place. Only then will Philippians four become a reality to you: *and the peace of God, which surpasses all understanding, will guard your hearts and minds through Christ Jesus* (Philippians 4:7).

ETERNAL PERSPECTIVE

I have learned that overcoming any loss is much easier when you choose to look at your situation from an eternal perspective. I call it, "seeing the big picture," or "putting things into perspective." As you heal from grief, and your emotional pain diminishes, it becomes much easier to see things as they really are. If you are going to see the big picture, it is important to remember that countless others have suffered pain and loss, and they came through victoriously without having lost their faith in God. In fact, it was their faith in God that saw them through.

The Book of Hebrews describes a great cloud of witnesses who kept the faith and set the example for other likeminded believers to follow in their footsteps (Hebrews 12:1). They endured great trials, tribulations, and hardships, yet they still managed to keep their trust and faith in God. It is written of them, "of whom the world was not worthy"

(Hebrews 11:38). Their faith kept them faithful in spite of their circumstances.

While in prison, the Apostle Paul was able to say that the things that happened to him actually turned out for the furtherance of the gospel. His God perspective allowed him to have joy in the midst of the worst circumstances of life. (Philippians 1:19-26)

DON'T SHRINK BACK

Our spiritual forefathers did not see the total outcome of their faith in their lifetime but they trusted God anyway. They were ordinary men and women who believed in God's faithfulness. They died in faith, yet believing. Hebrews 11:1 says, "Now faith is the substance of things hoped for, the evidence of things not seen." Your continued faith and trust in God is a major key to your recovery and healing, "For in him we live, and move, and have our being;" (Acts 17:28).

Our faithful forefathers did not shrink back in their faith when tragedies occurred. They kept pressing. They believed God. They kept leaning to God. They stayed connected to God. Hebrews 10:38 states, "Now the just shall live by faith: but if any man draw back, my soul shall have no pleasure in him."

God does not want you to give up (stop trusting), or pull away from Him (shrink back), or allow the pain of your loss to jeopardize the intimacy you share with Him. He knows you are hurting. He is the Father of all comforts who wants to comfort you in your troubles (1 Corinthians 1:3-4).

He has not forgotten you. As a shepherd carries a lamb, know that while you are grieving He is carrying you close to His heart (Isaiah 40:11). He has a plan for your full recovery and total healing.

GOOD REPORT

The early disciples obtained a good report by keeping the faith in spite of their pain and loss. Just like them, you too can obtain a good report if you keep the faith in spite of your loss. Fight the good fight of faith in order to hold on to that measure of faith that each individual has been given by God. Satan wants to steal your faith because he knows that without faith it is impossible to believe God, to please God, or to receive anything from God.

The Apostle Paul said, "I have fought a good fight, I have finished my course, I have kept the faith:" (2 Timothy 4:7). His faith in God was unshakable and undeniable! Paul used his faith not just to keep him on course, but also to help him finish his course. Going through any type of devastating loss does not exempt us, but rather challenges us to keep the faith like our spiritual ancestors did, Jesus being our great example.

Anyone who has suffered tragedy can receive great encouragement from the faith exemplified in the life of the Apostle Paul. He never allowed his trials and tribulations to affect his relationship with God. Because the Apostle Paul trusted in God's faithfulness, he readily chose to follow God's path for his life, no matter what he was facing.

He gave up his will for the will of the Father. Paul said in Acts 26:19, ". . . I was not disobedient unto the heavenly vision:" He kept obeying God through it all—He did not break faith with God when suffering became part of his reality. He did not allow Satan to avert God's plan for his life.

The Apostle Paul's faith was fixed on doing God's will—to him, any loss in this life would be counted as gain because it only served to deepen his love and commitment to God. It only made him want Heaven even more. He was totally sold out to God, understanding that his own purposes and personal desires in life had to become one with God.

And at the end of his life, I am sure that the Apostle Paul heard what all believers want to hear someday, "…Well done, thou good and faithful servant: thou has been faithful over a few things, I will make thy ruler over many things: enter thou into the joy of thy Lord." (Matthew 25:21)

CHOOSE THE GREATER

The Apostle Paul had chosen the greater (living a consecrated life) over the lesser (living carnally). The lesser does not allow room for God to work His purposes in your life, and it does not allow the challenges of this earthly life to make you better. Choosing the greater instead of the lesser is something you must decide on a day-to-day (sometimes moment-by-moment) basis.

My relationship with God has been the number one key to my recovery and healing. *As I have purposed in my heart to stay close to the Lord, and continue to believe His best for my life, He continues to pour healing into my heart.* God was working out His plan for my full recovery when I could not see it for myself, and when I was hurting too much to perceive what He was doing in my life.

For some time after losing my daughter, I could not see where God was taking me, but the Lord was working on my behalf, leading me into His perfect will for my life. I resisted for a while, but as I began to yield to this new path, my fellowship with God became sweeter and sweeter, and healing from grief became more and more of a reality in my life.

Because your relationship with God is vitally important to your recovery and your future, guard and protect it with all of your heart. Proverbs 4:23 says, "Keep thy heart with all diligence; for out of it are the issues of life." You must treasure your relationship with God like you would precious silver or gold, because it is something money cannot buy, and nothing in this life could ever replace it or even remotely compare to it.

YOUR TREASURE

God is a treasure, and He wants you to treasure Him above everything else—above any loss, no matter how dear it was to your heart. He wants you to treasure Him above ALL. Making God your treasure requires time spent alone with Him, time getting to know Him, and time seeking His face. It requires a heart like Jesus, whose attitude was always "... not my will, but thine, be done" (Luke 22:42).

The Apostle Paul prayed that you would have revelation into the height, depth, breadth, and length of God's love. He went on to pray that you would be rooted and grounded in His love (Ephesians 3:17-18). Paul desired that all believers would have insight into God's abounding love because he knew from personal experience its transforming power.

When the heartache of your loss becomes unbearable, when your life has been turned upside down with grief, when you are at the end of your rope, run into the loving arms of Faithful Father God. He wants to Father you while you are hurting. God is the perfect Father who will always care for you, love you, provide for you, protect you and do what is best for you. The more time you spend with God, the better you will feel and the more you will heal.

When you are tempted to become depressed over things in your life that seem out of control, ask yourself how much time have you spent in the secret place and in the presence of God. Your faith will keep your focus and worship on God. Spending time alone with God will keep you in that secret place, the inner court and beyond the veil into God's holy presence.

When you have done all you know to do, then there is but one thing left to do and that is to enter into His presence (the place were you belong) with songs of adoration, love and total surrender.

The lyrics of this song, "When I Look Into Your Holiness,"[4] will help to explain what I mean:

When I look into Your holiness
When I gaze into Your loveliness
When all things that surround me
Become shadows in the light of you
When I find the joy of reaching Your heart
When my will becomes
Enthroned in Your love
When all things that surround me
Become shadows in the light of you
I worship You, I worship You
the reason I live—is to worship You

When you have experienced a tragic loss, you must find a reason to go on with life—a reason to live. The Lord must become your reason to live. He is your source of comfort and healing. He is your all in all. Isaiah 41:13 states, "For I the LORD thy God will hold thy right hand, saying unto thee, Fear not; I will help thee." As the Holy Spirit reveals the Father's heart to you, as you open your heart to receive His love, and as you reciprocate love back to Him, emotional pain will not be able to move you away from the Father, it will only serve to move you closer to Him. Run to Him—He is waiting for you! Let Him lavish His love upon you!

GOD'S LOVE

You cannot earn God's love, for it is immeasurable and freely given without merit. You cannot earn what has already been given to you without any conditions or price tags. His love remains committed to you, no matter what tragedy has occurred in your life. Because of His great love for you, God will not desert you in your time of need.

> . . . for He [God] Himself has said, I will not in any way fail you nor give you up nor leave you without support. [I will] not, [I will] not, [I will] not in any degree leave you helpless nor forsake nor let [you] down (relax My hold on you)! [Assuredly not!] So we take comfort and are encouraged and confidently and boldly say, The Lord is my Helper: I will not be seized with alarm [I will not fear or dread or be terrified]. What can man do to me? Hebrews 13:5-6 (AMP)

God will always be there for you. He is your constant companion. Jesus said, "... lo, I am with you always, even unto the end of the world. Amen." (Matthew 28:20)

He will stay with you; He will support you, and help you through your time of grieving. He will be with you through every step of your recovery process to ensure that you make it to that promised place of healing and restoration.

Psalm 46:1 says, "God is our refuge and strength, a very present help in trouble."

If it had not been for the Lord's faithfulness and goodness in my life, my testimony might be different today. Staying connected to God caused my love for Him to deepen and the walls of pain in my life to gradually be removed.

The Lord began to stir within me a fresh faith as I relinquished my heartaches and disappointments into His loving hands. In 1 John 5:4 the Bible states, "For whatsoever is born of God overcometh the world: and this is the victory that overcometh the world, even our faith." Your faith has the power to overcome the pain of grief; therefore, you must not quit but you must go on in spite of your loss. Remember the principle that God will work through the negative to bring about the positive in your life. Allow God the time He needs to bring about a positive new future for you.

FAITH—A SPIRITUAL WEAPON

Do not let go of your faith because faith is a spiritual weapon against the pain of loss. Hebrews 10:35-36 instructs you to, "Cast not away therefore your confidence, which hath great recompense of reward. For ye have need of patience, that, after ye have done the will of God, ye might receive the promise." Keep your confidence in God and His promises to you, for there is a reward for your faith.

Exercising your faith will give you the courage to smile when you are hurting, to walk in forgiveness when you feel betrayed, to reach out to others when you feel empty and to fellowship with God when you feel numb.

Therefore, my advice to you if you are not progressing well in your grief journey is to begin to call those things that are not as though they were (Romans 4:17). Speak words of faith over your emotions. Decree the Word of God over your life.

Command the spirit of grief to leave you. Call forth the blessings of God into your life. Whatever you do, resist the temptation to stay stuck in grief or stuck in your past. Break free from the emotional chains of sorrow and pain. Step out of sin into sanctification.

The Bible says that those who sow in tears shall one day reap in joy. This is your hour for laughter and joy to spring forth. This is Your Time to Heal!

DREAM AGAIN
Psalm 126:1-3 says,

When the LORD turned again the captivity of Zion, we were like them that dream. Then was our mouth filled with laughter, and our tongue with singing: then said they among the heathen, The LORD hath done great things for them. The LORD hath done great things for us; whereof we are glad.

The pain of loss is one of the most devastating experiences you may ever encounter, but in the final analysis, you must remember that you may be struck down, but YOU get to decide whether you are struck out! You make the choice.

Being healed from grief takes time, but it also requires a daily choice and commitment to work through the pain of loss and grief and those unresolved issues from your past. Every crossing you make will bring you closer to healing and closer to the new thing that God has for you.

Remember that no matter what happens: Do not give up! Do not shrink back! Do not throw in the towel! Stand upright, square your shoulders back, and look toward your future with great expectation. Decree with your mouth that, "The Lord hath done great things for [me]!"

You can confidently say to yourself, "It's time to heal! It's time to dream again! Begin again! Live life again! Sing and shout for joy again!

For my God has been faithful to me!

Faithful to Me

In my moments of fear
Through every pain, every tear
There's a God whose been faithful to me.
When my strength was all gone,
When my heart had no song,
Still in love He's proved faithful to me.
Every Word He's promised is tried,
What I've thought was impossible
I see my God do,
He's been faithful to me.

Looking back, His love and mercy I see,
Though in my heart I've questioned,
Even failed to believe,
Yet He's been faithful to me.
When my heart looked away,
The many times I could not pray
The days I spent so selfishly,
Reaching out for what pleased me,
Even then, God was faithful to me.
Every time I come back to Him
He is waiting with open arms
And I see once again
He's been faithful to me.

Author: Unknown

JOURNAL NOTES

TRIBUTE

This book is a tribute to the life and memory of Stephanie Renee Deajon—beloved daughter, sister, friend, and woman of God. Your memory lives on.

STEPHANIE'S STORY

Stephanie Renee Deajon was born on May 8, 1974, just days before I turned eighteen years old. Her childhood was considered normal. She did all the things that kids her age did, but Stephanie always stood out from the crowd. As her younger brother Richard put it, "She represented herself very well."

Stephanie accepted Jesus Christ as her Lord and Savior at a church youth camp, and her heart for the Lord remained constant even when she was busy pursuing other things. Her love for the Lord was clearly woven into every season of her life. Her relationship with God did not start when she first discovered that she had diabetes, but had been ongoing and developing since she was young.

Stephanie always excelled in whatever she did and was fortunate to have had many wonderful experiences by the age of twenty-five. She had traveled to places most girls her age had only dreamed about; was involved in activities like modeling, acting, and cheerleading; excelled in academics; and attended the best private schools.

Material things, however, never went to her head; she was all about relationships, which was evident by her close inner circle of family and friends. One such relationship was with her younger brother. Stephanie and her brother Richard remained very close over the years.

One of the things Richard remembers most about Stephanie is how he could talk to her about anything. She listened, she cared, and she always understood. Just a few days before her death, Stephanie made a timely phone call to Richard, which reinforced their bond and love for each other.

The timing of that phone call, and his conversation with her, will be something that Richard will never forget because it helped him get through the pain of losing his sister.

She was especially close to her father, who loved her very much and made sure she had the best of everything. Stephanie was the apple of his eye and a daddy's girl, regardless of her age. Her relationship with her father was an important part of who she was, and that relationship was dear to her heart.

Stephanie was also the type of person everyone liked to be around. When asked what stood out most about her, Rebecca La Chapelle, Stephanie's cousin said this, "She never complained, she never asked for anything, she was always positive and upbeat, she always had a big smile on her face, and she always served. No one had to ask her to; it was just in her to serve."

Her sister Candace said, "Stephanie was one of a kind. When she was ill, she never complained about anything. I never knew anyone like her."

During Stephanie's last year in college, her physical health made a turn for the worst. It all began when she dropped about thirty pounds over a two-month period. Being extremely fatigued all the time, she knew that something was wrong in her body, even though the doctors were unable to discover what it was.

One day she became extremely ill, and her fiancé's mother advised her to go to the emergency room to get checked out. The nurses kept coming into the room to look at her, staring as if they had seen a ghost. Stephanie thought that their behavior was really strange. Apparently, the nurses could not get over how well she looked for someone who had come so close to death.

Stephanie was in diabetic shock and did not understand the extent of her physical condition. The emergency room doctor said that it was a miracle she was still alive since she had gone so long with her blood sugar level over 800 mg/dL (normal is about 100 mg/dL). The diagnosis—adult onset Type II diabetes!

With that diagnosis, life would become different for all of us, but especially for Stephanie. She had to eat healthier, exercise, monitor her blood sugar level, and take insulin shots every day. Implementing a new lifestyle was challenging enough, but there was more than just taking insulin shots, which Stephanie would soon discover.

My daughter went from living a carefree, happy life to a life controlled by insulin shots, needles, testing her blood several times a day, medicines, doctor's appointments, emergency room visits, and near death experiences.

One of the greatest blessings that came out of this crisis was the fact that it brought the two of us closer together. Through a series of events, Stephanie came to live with me for four years before she died. I believe that God gave us that time together.

Stephanie and her brother Richard had lived with their father and grandmother after their father and I divorced. By being with them only on weekends, it was very difficult for me to establish quality relationships with my children. I had missed so many important moments in both of their lives. It was not until years later that I was able to see how devastating the divorce had been for everybody concerned.

Unfortunately, I could not go back and change the past, but I prayed for many years that the Lord would restore my relationship with my children. And He did! The Lord gave me a second chance to be with Stephanie—a chance to get to know her, a chance for us to get to know each other, and a chance for us to be together.

After graduating from Xavier University in New Orleans, Louisiana, with a degree in chemistry, Stephanie came to live with me. She had so many great things going for her, and most of all, she had a wonderful future awaiting her—a new career, a new fiancée, and new friends. She had studied hard and was now on the threshold of a bright and prosperous future.

When the Lord brought Stephanie back into my life, I was so grateful. Then, approximately one year after Stephanie came to live with me, the Lord brought Candace back home. They were both an answer to many years of praying. During that time, my son Richard was living with his dad and going to college. We did not see him as much, but we stayed in touch and were together for special occasions and holidays. Restoration with my children was taking place and I could not be happier. I knew that only the hand of God could have restored my children back to me.

There was a mutual love between Stephanie and Candace, even though they had not grown up in the same household and did not have opportunities to see each other that often. Stephanie prayed for Candace during her sister's tough teenage years. She was very compassionate toward Candace and knew that she would do great things with her life. I was thankful for the time they had together. I believe that in ways only the two of them would know, Stephanie and Candace impacted each other's lives.

Stephanie and I thoroughly enjoyed each other's company, whether we were eating out, watching a movie, ministering together, or just hanging out around the house. We had fun being together, no matter what we were doing. The day that Candace's father brought her back to me, Stephanie and I were sitting in the living room praying for Candace.

Stephanie's graduation from Bible School was a tremendous milestone for her since she planned to someday work in the ministry full-time. After Bible School, Stephanie began working as a teacher in a Christian school. Even though she had originally gone to college to become a chemical engineer, her true calling was in the education field. In an interview with one of her students two months before her death, Stephanie was asked what she expected to get from teaching. She replied, "Well, I expected great things from teaching. I knew that it was an opportunity for me to impact the lives of young people." Another student made this comment about her, "Miss Deajon is an excellent role model and a faithful teacher, as well as a friend."

Over time, Stephanie's diabetes became more and more unmanageable. There were several instances when we found her slipping into a diabetic coma, almost at the point of death.

Before leaving the house one morning, her sister Candace went into Stephanie's bedroom to discover that she was not getting ready for work, but rather lay in bed almost unconscious. Candace quickly called 9-1-1 for help, and we were able to get her to the hospital just in time.

On another occasion, a police officer knocked on my front door and asked if I had a daughter named Stephanie Deajon. I stared speechlessly at the officer, totally petrified at what he might say next. He informed me that Stephanie's car had stalled in the middle of an expressway and that she was going in and out of consciousness. Not totally coherent, she thought the police were trying to harm her, so she somehow managed to lock the doors to her car. We loved teasing her about this later.

After we arrived at the scene that day, she recognized my voice and opened her car door. Thankfully, there was an astute nurse in the car behind her who quickly responded to the emergency. The nurse had just gone to the grocery store and had orange juice in her car. She gave her some orange juice and once again, Stephanie's life was spared.

Most of the time, Stephanie did not feel well in her body, but she usually did not say anything until we found her almost unconscious. She never complained of her constant nausea, migraine headaches, and sleepless nights. She would go from looking perfectly healthy to being near death. This is what is so terrible about diabetes—you can go from being at death's door to renewed health—all with one timely drink of orange juice.

Stephanie became ill while in Europe and was still not feeling well when we returned from our trip in March of 2000. She had flu-like symptoms and stayed home from work the following week to recuperate.

The day before Stephanie passed away, she was at home grading papers and catching up on all the paperwork that accompanied her job. It was early the next morning, around three o'clock that she died. Without a struggle, without a complaint, without even a simple good-bye, without burdening anyone, she quietly stepped out of our lives and into eternal life.

Several months after her funeral, I was looking through some of her things, and I realized that everything about her—the books she read, the friends she had chosen, the way she carried herself, and the choices she made in life—all reflected a beautiful young woman who loved God.

During her battle with diabetes, she chose to focus on her relationship with God. Her desire was to have a deeper walk with God. I believe that above anything or anyone else, it was her relationship with God, which sustained her and gave her that great inner strength she always had throughout her life.

As her mother, I give a good report of Stephanie Renee Deajon's life. Her final outcome was honorable and her home-going was not a tragedy but a wonderful celebration of someone who had loved God, loved life, loved people, and had left her mark on all who knew her.

Her best friend Tinera said it beautifully, "I believe Stephanie's whole existence was not about her, but the people she touched. She had the purest heart. She had a positive outlook on everything in life. She always put her best foot forward. She will never be forgotten!"

He Only Took My Hand

Last night while I was trying to sleep
My daughter's voice I did hear.
I opened my eyes and looked around,
But she did not appear.
She said, "Mama you've got to listen,
You've got to understand.
God didn't take me from you, Mama,
He only took my hand.
When I called out in my sleep that night,
The instant that I died,
He reached down and took my hand,
And pulled me to His side.
He pulled me up and saved me,
From the misery and pain.
My body was so ill inside,
I could never be the same.
My search is really over now,
I've found happiness within.

All the answers to my dreams,
And all that might have been.
I love you so and miss you so,
And I'll always be nearby.
My body's gone forever,
But my spirit will never die!
And so you must go on now,
Live one day at a time.
Just understand...
"God did not take me from you,
He only took my hand."

Author Unknown

APPENDIX

Father's Love Letter

My Child,

You may not know me, but I know everything about you
  ~ Psalm 139:1
I know when you sit down and when you rise up
  ~ Psalm 139:2
I am familiar with all your ways ~ Psalm 139:3
Even the very hairs on your head are numbered
  ~ Matthew 10:29-31
For you were made in my image ~ Genesis 1:27
In me you live and move and have your being ~ Acts 17:28
For you are my offspring ~ Acts 17:28
I knew you even before you were conceived
  ~ Jeremiah 1:4-5
I chose you when I planned creation ~ Ephesians 1:11-12

You were not a mistake, for all your days are written in my
   book ~ Psalm 139:15-16
I determined the exact time of your birth and where you
   would live ~ Acts 17:26
You are fearfully and wonderfully made ~ Psalm 139:14
I knit you together in your mother's womb ~ Psalm 139:13
And brought you forth on the day you were born
   ~ Psalm 71:6
I have been misrepresented by those who don't know me
   ~ John 8:41-44
I am not distant and angry, but am the complete expression
   of love ~ 1 John 4:16
And it is my desire to lavish my love on you ~ 1 John 3:1
Simply because you are my child and I am your Father
   ~ 1 John 3:1
I offer you more than your earthly father ever could
   ~ Matthew 7:11
For I am the perfect father ~ Matthew 5:48
Every good gift that you receive comes from my hand
   ~ James 1:17
For I am your provider and I meet all your needs
   ~ Matthew 6:31-33
My plan for your future has always been filled with hope
   ~ Jeremiah 29:11
Because I love you with an everlasting love
   ~ Jeremiah 31:3

My thoughts toward you are countless as the sand on the
   seashore ~ Psalm 139:17-18
And I rejoice over you with singing ~ Zephaniah 3:17
I will never stop doing good to you ~ Jeremiah 32:40
For you are my treasured possession ~ Exodus 19:5
I desire to establish you with all my heart and all my soul
   ~ Jeremiah 32:41
And I want to show you great and marvelous things
   ~ Jeremiah 33:3
If you seek me with all your heart, you will find me
   ~ Deuteronomy 4:29
Delight in me and I will give you the desires of your heart
   ~ Psalm 37:4
For it is I who gave you those desires ~ Philippians 2:13
I am able to do more for you than you could possibly imagine
   ~ Ephesians 3:20
For I am your greatest encourager
   ~ 2 Thessalonians 2:16-17
I am also the Father who comforts you in all your troubles
   ~ 2 Corinthians 1:3-4
When you are brokenhearted, I am close to you
   ~ Psalm 34:18
As a shepherd carries a lamb, I have carried you close to my
   heart ~ Isaiah 40:11
One day I will wipe away every tear from your eyes
   ~ Revelation 21:3-4

And I'll take away all the pain you have suffered on this earth ~ Revelation 21:3-4

I am your Father, and I love you even as I love my son, Jesus ~ John 17:23

For in Jesus, my love for you is revealed ~ John 17:26

He is the exact representation of my being ~ Hebrews 1:3

He came to demonstrate that I am for you, not against you ~ Romans 8:31

And to tell you that I am not counting your sins ~ 2 Corinthians 5:18-19

Jesus died so that you and I could be reconciled ~ 2 Corinthians 5:18-19

His death was the ultimate expression of my love for you ~ 1 John 4:10

I gave up everything I loved that I might gain your love ~ Romans 8:31-32

If you receive the gift of my son Jesus, you receive me ~ 1 John 2:23

And nothing will ever separate you from my love again ~ Romans 8:38-39

Come home and I'll throw the biggest party heaven has ever seen ~ Luke 15:7

I have always been Father, and will always be Father ~ Ephesians 3:14-15

My question is ~ Will you be my child? ~ John 1:12-13

I am waiting for you ~ Luke 15:11-32

. . . Love, Your Dad
Almighty God

*Father's Love Letter used by permission of Father Heart
Communications
Copyright 1999-2006 www.FathersLoveLetter.com

ADDENDUM I
POWER THOUGHTS ABOUT GRIEVING

- Focusing on the known instead of the unknown would become my pathway to healing.
- Experiencing a tragic loss does not have to destroy your life or cause you to become a bitter person.
- Getting beyond grief takes time, prayer, participation, education, and most of all lots of work.
- Put one foot in front of the other each and every day until you cross the finish line of grief.
- Remember that change is inevitable but growth is optional.
- Whatever it is that you lost initially came to you as a gift and blessing from God.
- You do not give thanks for your loss, but you are to remain thankful in spite of what you have lost. This is the heart attitude that God blesses.

- There are some things in life you have to go through in order to get through.
- Personal tragedies do not validate doctrine that is contrary to God's truth. The pain of loss and the intense emotions of grief can cause the most spiritually mature person to accept a belief or thought that is not of God.
- You may not verbalize what you believe, but you punish yourself inwardly by entertaining accusing thoughts about assumed shortcomings, failures, or mistakes from your past.
- With encouraging words should come the commitment to see that person through to the place of healing—speaking words of faith in God to comfort and heal them. Sometimes just sitting or crying with the one who is hurting helps them.
- Shame will always be an unspoken and invisible wall that stands between you and your emotional healing.
- Remember that you are a beautiful and wonderful work of art (a masterpiece), created by God in Christ Jesus. Being healed from grief requires that you see yourself the way God sees you.
- Knowing and applying the Word in every situation you face will be a vital key to your recovery from grief.
- Painful emotions do not go away simply because you refuse to face them.
- You will find that worship is part of the spiritual prescription for your healing.

- Finding the root cause of the pain is a significant part of the answer and a foundational step toward recovery.
- But keep in mind that grieving is only productive when healing is your ultimate goal.
- God always has His eyes on you and will continually watch over you like the silversmith watches over his silver.
- Our job is twofold: to understand what God is purposing to teach us in that particular season and to continually yield to the deeper work of the Holy Spirit.
- I knew that Jesus was telling me not to dwell on things that made me feel sad, and things that grieved my heart, but to look at the beauty of life all around.
- Complete emotional healing will not take place until you are walking in a place of total forgiveness, continually guarding your heart against anger, offense, and bitterness, while at the same time keeping it pure, tender, and pliable before God.
- Forgiveness is a process not an event.
- Being honest about how you feel removes the power that painful emotions can have over you and is another positive step toward acceptance and healing.
- The decision to let go of anger and unforgiveness will play a significant role in your ability to grieve your losses and move on with your life.
- Forgiveness opens a spiritual door through which God is able to begin His restoration process in your life.

- The deepest level of forgiveness comes from the heart. A wounded heart is healed when you forgive at the deepest level, and that is why it is so important not to harbor unforgiveness while you are grieving.
- As you purpose in your heart to stay close to the Lord, and continue to believe His best for your life, He will continue to pour healing into your heart.

ADDENDUM II
PRAYERS THAT HEAL A GRIEVING HEART

Salvation Prayer

If you would like to pray the prayer of salvation, or you want to rededicate your life to the Lord, please pray the following prayer:

Dear God,

I believe that Jesus Christ is the Son of God. I believe that He died on the cross and He rose again from the dead and is seated with You in Heaven. I believe that one day He will come back for me as He promised.

Jesus, please forgive me of my sins and come into my heart. I give you my life and ask you to fill me with your Holy Spirit today. Thank you for saving me, healing me and giving me new life. In Jesus' name, I pray, Amen.

Chapter 2:

Questioning God Prayer

Heavenly Father, You said in Your Word to ask, seek, and knock. I ask You today to give me understanding about what happened. Help me to see what happened through Your eyes of love and not through the pain and heartache that I am feeling.

You said in Your Word that I could have the knowledge of Your will with all spiritual wisdom and understanding. Lord, I ask for wisdom today in everything that I do and say. I confess that Your Word is a lamp unto my feet and a light unto my path.

Lord, give me peace in my heart. I do acknowledge that You are Sovereign. Help me to accept my loss and help me to trust and accept the things that I do not understand. I want to release it all to You, Heavenly Father.

Open my eyes to see what You see, to hear what You hear, to say what You say, and to think Your thoughts. I lay all of my questions at your feet, trusting You in all of this.

Fill me with Your Spirit today, Lord. I receive Your grace, Your understanding, Your peace, Your love, and Your strength, in Jesus' name. Amen.

Chapter 3:

Processing Grief Prayer

Dear Heavenly Father,

I come before you in the name of Jesus. I ask you to help me with the pain I am feeling because of losing _____.

Please help me to see things through your eyes, and help me to keep a grateful heart in spite of everything that has happened.

Your Word says to be strong in the Lord and the power of his might. I decree that I am strong in you and in the power of your might (Ephesians 6:10).

Holy Spirit, fill me and empower me to grieve and mourn according to God's Word. Your Word says that "Blessed are they that mourn: for they shall be comforted" (Matthew 5:4). I receive your comfort now.

I receive your grace and I confess that your grace is sufficient for me; and that in my weakness your strength is made perfect (1 Corinthians 12:9).

I confess that I can do all things through Christ who strengthens me (Philippians 4:13). I confess that no weapon formed against me shall prosper (Isaiah 54:17). I confess that I always triumph in Christ Jesus (1 Corinthians 2:14).

Lord, I ask you to heal me from this pain and make me whole again. I receive my healing now, in Jesus' name. Amen.

Chapter 4:

Struggling with Emotions Prayer

Dear Lord, I come before you in the name of Jesus. I humble my heart before you and ask you to forgive me for believing lies about myself. You said in your Word that there is no condemnation for those who are in Christ Jesus. Christ lives in me; therefore I refuse to listen to the voice of condemnation, guilt, and self-hatred any longer.

I resist the enemy and release myself from all negative emotions. They do not belong to me. I send them back to the pit where they came from.

Lord, I ask you to forgive me for hating myself, or blaming myself or anyone else for what has happened. I understand that no one is perfect except Jesus and I understand that you do not require perfection from me; you accept me just as I am. You said in your Word that you are looking for a humble and contrite heart from which you would never despise nor turn away.

I confess that I do not have a spirit of fear but of love, power, and a calm, sound mind. Dear Lord, establish my thoughts and heal my damaged emotions by the Word of your power.

Help me to also accept what has happened without blaming or condemning anyone. Purify my mind, my heart, and my soul. Renew a right spirit within me. Help me to be strong and not give up, and help me to keep my eyes stayed upon you that I may have perfect peace always, in Jesus' name. Amen.

Grief Emotions Prayer

Dear Heavenly Father,

I give all of my feelings and emotions to you, Lord. Please forgive me for thinking negative thoughts and believing lies from the enemy. I renounce every thought in my life that is not of you. I confess that I have the mind of Christ and that the washing of Your Word renews my thinking. I confess that I am anxious for nothing and in all things, through prayer and supplication, I will make my requests known unto you and the peace of God that surpasses all understanding will rule and reign in my heart and mind in Christ Jesus. Thank you for filling my mind with peace.

Lord, you said in Romans 12:2 not to be conformed to this world but be transformed by the renewing of my mind that I may know the good, pleasing, and perfect will of God. I confess that my mind is renewed, my thinking is clear, and that I know your perfect will for my life. I receive it now in Jesus' name.

Thank you for healing my emotions and healing my heart. I confess that I am strong in the Lord and the power of your might. I confess that I can do all things through Christ who strengthens me. Holy Spirit, fill me to overflowing—fill me without measure that I might triumph in all things today.

Thank you for helping me—I claim victory over my life, in Jesus' name, Amen.

Chapter 5:

Inner Healing Prayer

Dear Heavenly Father,

Search me, O God, and know my heart: try me and know my thoughts: And see if there be any wicked way in me, and lead me in the way everlasting (Psalm 139:23-24).

Holy Spirit, I welcome you into my life. As you search my heart, show me what is keeping me from being the person you want me to be—show me what is keeping me from being a happy person.

I ask you to heal me of past hurts—heal the wounds that have kept me in bondage. Help me to face my past and let go of this _____ (specific hurts) and unforgiveness. Forgive me for holding on to these hurts—take away the painful memories that linger in my mind. Take away the power that they have had over me.

I forgive _____ for the hurts they caused in my life. I release them from any debt I thought they owed me and I put them now into your hands. I repent of _____; please forgive me, Lord. Thank you for cleansing my heart from this unrighteousness.

Jesus, come into my heart. Let me see you in every hurt of my life. I want to hear your voice and feel your touch. Give me the freedom and peace I so yearn for. I close my eyes now—I am picturing you, Jesus, sitting on a rock along the water's edge. Take me with you, Jesus, as you walk along the Sea of Galilee. Show me beautiful things from the works of your hands.

Fill me today with your joy, your peace, and your love, Lord Jesus. I love you with all my heart. I surrender my all to you and I receive your healing touch today, in Jesus' name. Amen.

Chapter 6:

Forgiveness Prayers
Anger/Disappointment with God

Dear Lord, I see that I have misjudged you and blamed you for things that you did not do. I choose to stop doing this. I ask you to forgive me for my sin against you. I know and affirm that you are a good God and that you want only the best for me, which is to transform me into the image of Jesus Christ.

I agree with you that you are in charge of my life, and that everything that happens to me is for my development and maturing into a son/daughter, able to rule and reign with you in eternity.

I will put the blame where it really belongs, on myself and on Satan. I will stop being a blame shifter, but will be responsible for my own life, under the guidance and control of the Holy Spirit.

Thank you, Lord, for new freedom today, and for a renewed relationship with you. I receive both of these in the name of Jesus Christ. Amen!

Forgiving Others

Father, you have made it clear that you require me to forgive. You desire the healing and freedom for me that forgiveness brings. So today, I choose to forgive all who have set me up to enter into sin and all who have hurt me. I choose to release them, each and every one. I let go of all judgments against them, and I let go of all punishments for them that I have harbored in my heart. I turn all of this, and all of them, over to you.

Holy Spirit, I thank you for working forgiveness into my life, for giving me the grace I need to forgive, and for continuing to enable me to forgive. In Jesus' name, Amen!

Asking God's Forgiveness

Father, now that I have forgiven all others, I thank you that I can now come to receive your forgiveness. So I come to you, through the shed blood of Jesus and the power of His Cross, asking you to forgive me of all of my sins. I acknowledge and take responsibility for each and every time I have violated your commandments, as well as for the iniquity that is in my heart.

Holy Spirit, thank you for working forgiveness into my life, for healing me, and for cleansing me from all unrighteousness. Thank You, Father, for restoring me to fellowship with you. In the name of Jesus Christ, I pray. Amen!

Forgiving Myself

Father, because you have forgiven me, I choose to forgive myself and to release myself from all accusations, judgments, hatred, slander, mistakes, stupidity, and falling short of the mark. I choose to accept myself just as I am because you accept me. I choose to love myself because you love me. I expect to begin to like myself.

Holy Spirit, I ask you, I give you permission, and I expect you to work your work of sanctification in me. I fully embrace this truth and look forward to working with you so I can be changed into the image of Christ. In the name of Jesus Christ I pray. Amen!

*Forgiveness Prayers taken from *Restoring the Foundations*
Copyright 2001, Proclaiming His Word, Inc.

SUGGESTED RESOURCES

MINISTRIES

1. Restoring the Foundations
   Healing House Network
   Chester & Betsy Kylstra
   2849 Laurel Park Hwy
   Hendersonville NC 28739
   800-291-4706 or 828-696-9075
   office@HealingHouse.org
   http://www.healinghouse.org/index.html
2. Theophostic Prayer Ministry
   Dr. Ed Smith
   PO Box 489
   Campbellsville KY 42719
   270-465-3757
   phostic@kyd.net
   www.theophostic.com
3. Jeff Floyd Ministries
   Jefferson H. & Norma R. Floyd

PO Box 572
   Noblesville, IN 46060
   Fax: 317-816-9134
   Email: jhf72934@aol.com
   www.jfloydministries.org
4. Communion with God Ministries
   Mark & Patti Virkler
   3792 Broadway St
   Buffalo NY 14227-1123
   716-681-4896
   cwg@cwgministries.org
   www.cwgministries.org
5. The National Self-Help Clearing House
   (They will help you find a self-help group for your particular need)
   365 5th Avenue, Suite 3300
   New York, NY 10016
   212-817-1822
   www.selfhelpweb.org
6. The Compassionate Friends, Inc
   P.O. Box 3696
   Oak Brook, IL 60522
   Toll-Free: 877-969-0010
   Phone: 630-990-0010
   www.compassionatefriends.org
7. Beth Moore
   Living Proof Ministries

P.O. Box 840849
Houston, Texas 77284
1-888-700-1999
281-859-1375
lproof.org

DORIS LANG MINISTRIES, INC.

Faithful is He who calls you, and He also will bring it to pass.
I Thessalonians 5:24 (NASB)

For *Your Time To Heal* workshops, contact us:

Doris Lang
P.O. Box 500081
Austin, TX 78750
info@dorislang.com
www.dorislang.com

BIBLIOGRAPHY

Chapter 2
1. Guyon, Jeanne. *Experiencing the Depths of Jesus Christ*. Jacksonville, FL: SeedSowers Publishing, 1981:35.
2. Niebuhr, Reinhold, *The Serenity Prayer*.

Chapter 3
1. Wright, H. Norman. *Recovering from the Losses of Life*. Grand Rapids, MI: Revell, 2001.
2. The Merriam-Webster Dictionary, Springfield, MA, 1997, s.v. "grief".
3. Peterson, Lorraine. *Restore My Soul*.Colorado Springs, CO: Navpress, 2000:9.
4. Parachin, Victor M. *Grief Relief*. St. Louis, MO: Chalice Press, 1991:17, 36.
5. Davies, Laurie. *Brochure - 25Years of Saving Lives – MADD*. Driven / Fall 2006, www.madd.org: 9.
6. Cloud, PhD. Henry and Townsend, PhD. John.

God Will Make a Way. Brentwood, TN: Integrity Publishers, 2006:192.

Chapter 4
1. The Merriam-Webster Dictionary, Springfield, MA, 1997, s.v. "condemnation".
2. Kylstra, Chester & Betsy. *Restoring the Foundations. An Integrated Approach to Healing Ministry.* Hendersonville, NC: Proclaiming His Word, Inc, 2001:155.
3. Littauer, Florence. *Silver Boxes.* Nashville, TN: Thomas Nelson, 1989.
4. Fossum, Merle & Mason, Marilyn. *Facing Shame.* New York, NY: W. W. Norton & Company, 1986.
5. Smedes, Lewis B. *Shame and Grace.* New York, NY: HarperSanFrancisco, Zondervan Publishing House, 1993:107.
6. The Merriam-Webster Dictionary, Springfield, MA, 1997, s.v. "fear".
7. The Merriam-Webster Dictionary, Springfield, MA, 1997, s.v. "resist".

Chapter 5
1. Shakespeare, William, *Hamlet*, Act 1, sc iii.
2. Stapleton, Ruth Carter. *The Gift of Inner Healing.* Waco, TX: Word Books, 1976:10.

Chapter 6

1. The Merriam-Webster Dictionary, Springfield, MA, 1997, s.v. "forgiveness".
2. Floyd, Jefferson H. *Neither Give Place.* Longwood, FL: Xulon Press, 2002:128.
3. Hipp, Earl. *Help for the Hard Times.* Center City, MN: Hazelden, 1995.
4. The Merriam-Webster Dictionary, Springfield, MA, 1997, s.v. "defilement".
5. The Merriam-Webster Dictionary, Springfield, MA, 1997, s.v. "clean".

Chapter 7

1. *The New Strong's Exhaustive Concordance of the Bible*, Nashville, TN, 1990, s.v. "faithful".
2. The Merriam-Webster Dictionary, Springfield, MA, 1997, s.v. "faithful".
3. Lemme, Helen, "Turn Your Eyes upon Jesus," Singspiration, Inc. 1922, 1950.
4. Perrin, Wayne & Cathy, "When I Look into Your Holiness," Integrity's Hosanna! Music, 1980.

Printed in the United States
115904LV00001B/100-138/A

9 781602 667891